The Footpaths of Britain

The Footpaths of Britain

A Guide to Walking in England, Scotland and Wales

Michael Marriott

Foreword by John Hillaby

Queen Anne Press
Macdonald & Co
London & Sydney

An Adkinson Parrish Book

First published in 1981
in Great Britain
by Queen Anne Press,
a division of Macdonald & Co
(Publishers) Ltd., Maxwell House,
74 Worship Street,
London EC2A 2EN

Second impression 1983

ISBN 0362 00544 3   hardback
ISBN 0356 10126 6   paperback

Phototypesetting and colour and
black-and-white origination by
Siviter Smith Limited, Birmingham

Printed and bound in Spain by
Printer industria gráfica SA,
Sant Vicenç dels Horts, Barcelona
D.L.B. 17260-1981

Contents

Foreword

Winter walking in the Brecon Beacons, tough, exhilarating, but only to be attempted in such conditions by experienced hill-walkers with the proper equipment.

By sheer good luck I managed to buy a small stone-built cottage in the very heart of the North Yorkshire Moors where the sense of space is tremendous and the views are for ever. Within a quarter of an hour I can reach the central section of one of the most famous walks in the country, the Lyke Wake Walk, an ambulatory switch-back that clings to the very rim of the Dales. Time and time again I have watched walkers striding along that heavily trampled pathway which, end to end, extends for nearly 50 miles. Their gait is fascinating. Walkers can roughly be divided into plodders, those who crash straight through mud and streamlets as if unaware of what lies underfoot, and the light footmen and women who almost subconsciously pick their way around obstacles and reach their destination with their footwear fairly clean.

The difference is a matter of balance. The well-conditioned walker puts to good use some of the dramatic arrogance of the trained actor who, though tired after a long performance, sweeps forward to the curtain for his final bow as if he were treading on air. Watch the walker's arms, his feet. They scarcely seem to touch the ground. Upright walking is one of the outstanding differences between man and his ape-like forbears. It is a unique activity in which, step by step, the body teeters on the edge of catastrophe.

Walking is a way of reviving a very old way of life once shared by mendicant friars, beggers, bards, pilgrims and travelling artisans. As Henry James remarked, landscape is character and walking–which is a form of touching–is like making love to the landscape and letting it return that love throughout your whole body. The rewards abound, and there is a dragon-slaying feeling in distance done.

Long-distance walking, I maintain, is a fine art and, as in other arts, the apprentice should be well-tutored and, at the beginning, acutely conscious of what he or she is doing. It is not just a matter of pushing off into the country with or without a pack on your back. How fast should you walk? I suggest quite slowly at the start. It is necessary to recognize what I have called the three gears of pedestrianism. The first is Ambulatory Neutral, the pace for the first two or three miles when, if necessary, you should stop, repeatedly, and adjust your straps, belts and laces to ensure that absolutely nothing is chafing or fastened too tightly or causing the least bit of discomfort. If not attended to immediately a slightly crumpled stocking or a piece of grit the size of a pin head can provoke a blister the size of a thumb. Laughable as it may sound, it is important, too, to arrange your toes before pulling on your boots or shoes. Each one should lie perfectly flat, and no toe nail should protrude even by a mere fraction of an inch. For many people the little toe in particular tends to curl partly over the one next to it; if that happens it can be badly bruised and painful after a few miles of brisk pounding. Then, when all is in good order, you can step up to Normal Cruising speed, switching over, if you are in good form, to Ambulatory Overdrive. Like love, this is difficult to describe. It can only be experienced. It is a super-charged, almost mystical form of motion that only seasoned long-distance solitaries can fully experience.

Idyllic walking country in the Black Mountains not far from Offa's Dyke Path.

Towards nightfall or near the summit of a hill, which, of course, you will have attacked by contouring, you will be less–or more–than human if you do not experience a sort of dragging sensation in the small of your back. At that moment the trick is to bend forward from your hips upward without, if possible, losing your balance or breaking your stride. The relief can be something almost magical. If at such times you have doubts about why you are walking instead of being hauled around by something noisy on wheels you may care to remember one of my many memorable encounters on a walk from the North Sea to the Mediterranean.

In the great city of Metz on the fringe of Lorraine, I met a rich young man who said that all his life he had wanted to travel alone on foot as I did, but that somehow he could never make up his mind to begin. What made it all so worthwhile? After talking and drinking until two in the morning I thought I had got pretty close to the heart of the matter. Independence, I said. Walking meant no pre-ordained schedules, no hanging about waiting for transport, for other people to arrive and depart. Alone with a pack on your back you can set off anywhere at any time and change your plans on the way if you want to. Looking around his pleasant apartment, I remarked that of course it depended on what one did for a living. Could he get away for a few weeks? He shook his head, slowly. No, he said, it was difficult. In five words that brought a curious kind of chill he said, 'I run a travel agency'. A bleak silence followed. I enjoyed his coffee and left. The next morning, miles away in the handsomely named high forest of Ars-Laquenexy, I strode on towards Strasbourg, alone and free.

That was a good walk of about twelve hundred miles. In this book, within relatively few pages, a professional offers you the key to contentment in your own country. Even to turn its pages is for me, an old-timer, a constant reminder of what most of us yearn for: the earned experiences and destinations of those who do their travelling under their own power.

John Hillaby

Best Foot Forward

Walkers tackling a mountain path in Snowdonia (see page 151), a popular holiday area with pleasant routes to suit all walking tastes.

It is a curious quirk of human nature that in our over-mechanized society walking for pleasure is an acquired art. Admittedly, there are a few pedestrians who start early and stride their way healthily through life, usually to a ripe old age. For most of us, however, a few hundred yards with the dog or a stroll in the park is as much as we care to step out during day-to-day life.

Significantly, nowadays more and more people are acquiring that art and are deriving enormous enjoyment from it. Straight away, it must be said that there are times when even the most dedicated walkers question their enthusiasm. Anyone who has been caught in a high-country storm, cold, soaked to the skin, tired beyond belief and with several miles of muddy track ahead, will know the feeling. Fortunately, such experiences are rare. And, unpleasant though they are at the time, afterwards they tend to be the most remembered, recalled with what amounts to a grudging affection.

In any case, the benefits of walking far outweigh these temporary discomforts. To begin with, there is the sheer relief of mobility without the motor car. Then there is the satisfaction that comes from achievement. Everyone who has completed a long walk or, better still, has tramped from one end to the other of a long-distance path will know the splendid glow of well-being that lingers long after the return home. Above all, there is a renewed sense of vigour: irrespective of your age, sex and (within reason) your state of health, regular walking can only be healthy exercise, perhaps even a literal life-preserver.

Along with these physical and mental benefits comes the reward of getting to know the countryside and the natural world at first hand, something that is impossible if you remain encapsulated in a car. For those willing to use their feet, Britain can hardly be bettered by any other

SYMBOLS USED ON THE MAPS

	Main Maps	Detail Maps	The Best of British Walks Maps
Footpaths			
Motorways			
A Roads			
B Roads			
Railways and Stations			
Canals			
Country Boundaries			
County Boundaries			
Large Towns	Maidstone	Guildford	Sevenoaks
Small Towns	Midhurst	Westerham	Arundel
Villages		Cocking	Rackham
Youth Hostels	▲ Tanners Hatch	▲ Holmbury St Mary	▲ Tomintoul
Physical Features		Cocking Down	Beeding Hill
Places of Interest		☐ Wiston Park	☐ Chanctonbury Ring
Ancient Roads			
Ancient Walls and Dykes			
National Parks			
Areas of Outstanding Natural Beauty			

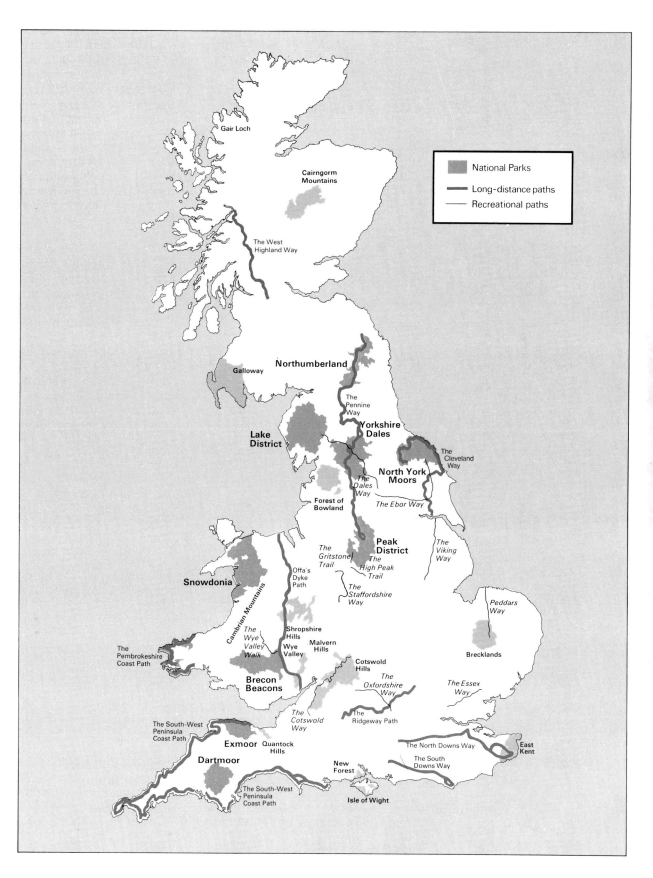

National Parks
Long-distance paths
Recreational paths

Gair Loch

Cairngorm
Mountains

The West
Highland Way

Northumberland

Galloway

The
Pennine
Way

Lake
District

Yorkshire
Dales

The
Cleveland
Way

North York
Moors

The
Dales
Way

The Ebor Way

Forest of
Bowland

The
Gritstone
Trail

Peak
District

The
High Peak
Trail

The
Viking
Way

Snowdonia

Offa's
Dyke
Path

The
Staffordshire
Way

Cambrian Mountains

The
Wye
Valley
Walk

Shropshire
Hills

Malvern
Hills

Peddars
Way

The
Pembrokeshire
Coast Path

Wye
Valley

Cotswold
Hills

Brecklands

Brecon
Beacons

The
Oxfordshire
Way

The Essex
Way

The South-West
Peninsula
Coast Path

The
Cotswold
Way

The
Ridgeway Path

The North Downs Way

East
Kent

Exmoor

Quantock
Hills

Dartmoor

New
Forest

The South
Downs Way

The South-West
Peninsula
Coast Path

Isle of Wight

The Pennine Way, the first of Britain's long-distance paths and still claimed by many as the toughest, grandest and most romantic of them all.

land. The magnificent network of footpaths, more than 100,000 miles long in total, offers an enthralling variety of landscape that is always interesting, often beautiful and sometimes breathtaking.

Walking in Britain has yet another fascination. Many footpaths have been established for hundreds of years. Some are older still. The Ridgeway across Wiltshire and Berkshire was in use well over two thousand years ago, for instance, and on Hadrian's Wall we can walk along the same route as centurions patrolling the frontier of the powerful Roman Empire.

The first footpaths were used for transporting goods such as salt, a commodity once more precious than gold. Other routes were first walked by pilgrims. Whenever possible these early paths ran on high ground, avoiding the uncleared forest in the valleys. As the landscape was gradually tamed, most notably–and dramatically–by the Romans, lowland tracks largely replaced hill-top paths. These gradually grew over the centuries into a well-trodden, nationwide system of agricultural paths, many of which were finally paved for wheeled traffic. The hill-top paths meanwhile fell into disuse and remained untrodden in the main except by drovers and pilgrims, until the new nomads–the leisure walkers–rediscovered them centuries later.

In the 1930s, as more and more people sought relief from city air in green spaces, long-distance walking began to revive. Ever since the Second World War, successive governments have acknowledged the important part played by the countryside in providing fresh air for a largely urban population. Public access to the countryside was not won immediately, however. In 1949, every local authority was obliged to prepare and maintain a map of local footpaths and bridleways. Sixteen years later, after quite some struggles, the Pennine Way, the first of the long-distance paths, was opened, and by 1980 there were no less than nine, with several more in active preparation. Much of this work is now in the hands of the Countryside Commission, one government body that all outdoor enthusiasts should bless.

My aim in the following pages is to pass on in words and pictures not just practical information but also something of the deep and sustained pleasure of exploring Britain's footpaths–a rewarding bonus after twenty-five years of writing about outdoor pursuits. Some of the major routes I have walked in their entirety, among them the Pennine Way, the South-West Peninsula Coast Path and Offa's Dyke Path. Others–the Pembrokeshire Coast Path, the South Downs Way and the Cleveland Way–I have come to know well through repeated visits. And while I cannot claim to have walked every single mile mentioned, I have tramped most of the scenic stretches.

In addition, I have visited almost all the other parts of Britain where the walker may stretch himself, often far away from any of the official long-distance paths. The results of those trips form the second part of this book: a personal selection–and it must be a selection, if only for reasons of space–of the best walks throughout the country. Some are almost as demanding, and require almost as much experience, as the long-distance paths; others are less taxing but none the less worthwhile and enjoyable. Some of the areas mentioned are celebrated walking country, crossed by beautiful and spectacular footpaths. Others are less well known but equally fascinating: Thetford Forest in the Suffolk/Norfolk border country, the Highlands-in-miniature in Galloway and the Shropshire Hills.

Finally, I include a gazetteer which lists the shorter recreational paths and country parks that offer a pleasant half day's or day's walking when there is neither time nor opportunity for anything more challenging.

I hope the reader will find this diverse coverage of practical value. The book does not set out to be a detailed footpath survey, however, for many such publications, both on the long-distance paths and on other walking areas, are already available. These mile-by-mile guides are suitable for use quite literally in the field and complement those marvellous and meticulous works of art, the Ordnance Survey maps. This book is rather an appetite-whetter, a countrywide survey of all that Britain has to offer those prepared to put their best feet forward. I hope it will spark your enthusiasm for exploration and help you to get the most from your expeditions. In addition, I hope it will help you to recall past ventures, some idyllic, some no doubt grim, all assuredly memorable.

One thing is certain. A walk of a decent length will always be a genuine adventure, providing more to see and hear than a car journey ten times as long. And at the end you will feel true achievement: an achievement better experienced than described and one that, as with anything really worthwhile, has had to be earned.

Good waymarking can usually be taken for granted nowadays on all the long-distance paths and in many other walking areas. None the less, experienced walkers never venture far without map and compass, certainly never into hills or moorland. Top and centre are typical signs that walkers may encounter, while the bottom sign reminds us that we are but visitors in the countryside.

The Walker's Basic Needs

Walkers are indeed fortunate, for their needs are small in comparison with those of more sophisticated pursuits. Walking is the cheapest method of travel in the world. There is a price, of course, but the coinage is time and modest physical effort. Given regular practice and a little determination, walking quickly becomes easy, then enjoyable, and eventually an essential part of your life. Desultory enthusiasm, however, is not sufficient for the kind of walking described in this book. A long-term plan is necessary, with some worthwhile goal: walking the full length of the Pennine Way or Offa's Dyke Path, for example, or even the trans-Europe Path from the Channel to the Mediterranean.

Getting into shape

There need be nothing fanatical about the physical preparation necessary to become a genuine walker. If, like most of us, you are a little overweight, sluggish and slightly unfit, the remedy is easy and painless; so long as you have a worthy goal it will also be enjoyable.

All that is required is a modest training programme to expand the capacity of your heart, lungs and muscles. Begin with thirty minutes of brisk local walking each day. If that seems rather much, try to fit in two fifteen-minute bouts, walking to the station and back every day, perhaps, or setting aside some of the lunch hour. Keep fit by taking this daily walk in summer and winter, come rain or shine, and supplement it at weekends with forays of two or three hours, preferably across undulating countryside.

Modest abstinence will almost certainly be beneficial as well. If you are overweight, cut down a little on sugar and carbohydrates. Nothing drastic is necessary, just enough to shed the obvious surplus. Instant fitness should not be expected from all this. But a year of slightly more active, slightly less indulgent living will reward you with the rediscovered glow of good health and renewed agility and litheness. If walking was once a physical chore it will now be a pleasant, natural and effortless routine, as essential to your well-being as food and sleep.

There are those who catch the fitness fever badly, supplementing daily walks with isometrics and press-ups, switching to a macro-diet, stopping drinking, smoking and most of life's other little enjoyments. This may result in rude

health but it is a bore both for yourself and for those around you. Beware of going over the top: a tune-up, not a total transformation, is the aim.

While walking is a cheap pursuit, it is a pursuit—not quite a sport, but close enough to require a certain amount of special clothing and equipment. Once you have embarked on your fitness programme you will soon have to start considering what you need.

Footwear

It goes without saying that footwear is most important of all. And here one cannot be dogmatic. Some young walkers wear nothing stouter than training boots whatever the season or terrain, immune, so it seems, to wet feet and blisters. Others, who cannot tolerate being restricted around the ankles, opt for stout walking shoes. Some ex-army types are happy in ammunition boots, and a minority even tramps blissfully in wellingtons.

Here, however, I am concerned with

A comfortable sweater (preferably all-wool) or an anorak, slacks or walking trousers (not jeans) and stout boots are the proper equipment for the hills. Whatever you wear, it must be comfortable and should not restrict you in any way.

what most people choose to wear, the orthodox natural-leather hill-walking boot. The salient requirements of any boot—from the modestly priced to the bespoke—are substantial insulation between your feet and the ground (especially if you intend to carry a ruck-sack); a non-slip sole; good ankle support; and efficient weather-keeping properties.

A visit to any well-stocked sports equipment shop will reveal the large number of different brands of walking boot available. Take time to decide which suits you best; ask the assistants for advice (many of them are keen outdoor enthusiasts themselves) and try on as many different pairs as you need to.

Although the lighter, cheaper boots

A group of walkers, obviously expecting rain, discuss their route. Hill-walking is best done with a companion, better still in a group of three: in case of accident, one can go for help while the other stays with the injured walker. (Incidentally, the tent poles on the right are *not* well stowed.)

Boots should be sturdy and have shanked soles, as shown on the right; thick wool socks are also essential. The size of the rucksack depends on the length of the walk.

may be useful for beginners, most serious walkers will prefer at least a medium-priced, sturdier model. There are a number of characteristics for which to look out. A sewn-in tongue, which helps to keep water out, is very important, as is adequate, strategically placed padding. A minimum of leather pieces and stitching ensures a maximum of proofing; the upper should be made from one piece of leather only, with the addition perhaps of a central heel strip.

The best boots have an internal toe-block to give protective rigidity and a 'shanked' sole to prevent over-flexing; the instep is stiffened by a hickory wedge inserted between the sole and the upper. The one-piece sole and heel should be made of a hard-wearing, non-slip composite. Such patterns are described as 'self-shedding'; cloggy mud tends to work outwards, worm-like, as you walk, a great virtue when you are struggling through sticky mud.

On cheaper models the impact-adhesive sole and heel is directly attached to the upper. This makes repairs very difficult and in any case is less satisfactory than the design of more expensive boots, in which a leather sub-sole is placed between the sole and the upper. A high-pressure adhesive system retains the layers and no visible screws or stitching are employed. For repair, the sole and heel piece is removed from the leather sub-platform and a replacement piece is impacted.

The most expensive boots have refinements such as hinged tongues, screwed and stitched soles and crimped closure ankle bands. But you pay for such extras in both price and weight.

No matter which make of boot you select, the fit must be as near perfect as possible. As you walk your feet expand, often quite considerably. To compensate for this, you must think oversize. A full size up from your normal shoe fitting will probably be necessary. The surplus will be taken up with thick oversocks; Norwegian ragg wool, either ankle- or knee-length, are the most popular.

When you are trying boots on, unlace them and thrust your foot well forward into the toe end. If you can then slip your index finger fairly easily between your heel and the rear wall of the boot the fit is satisfactory.

First steps in new boots, particularly if you are unused to wearing the shanked kind, may well be a trifle strange, and you may even feel a little like a deep-sea diver. However, it is this very feature that will ensure tireless comfort when you take to the footpaths. Shanked boots tend to make you walk slightly more slowly and deliberately, with a definite heel-first action. This soon becomes perfectly natural and makes a marked difference to the ease with which you can cover the miles, even over rough country.

When you have bought your boots, break them in gently by wearing them at home and for local walking. It may well take some time for your feet to feel really 'at home' in them, and it is inadvisable to embark on a major walk in brand-new boots.

Apply a generous coat of preservative to new boots and repeat the process a week or two later. Most boot leathers are already supple and only

Basic equipment for even a day's walk: rucksack, map and compass and quick-energy food supply.

Modern brew-up sets are very light and provide welcome hot drinks at strategic moments–well worth the little effort needed to carry them.

need a little dressing. If you use too much too often, the boots may become over-soft; the ankle support will weaken and the stitching will begin to 'work'. This in turn will make the stitch holes larger, giving water a chance to enter. As a rule, six applications of dressing a year are sufficient.

Acid is the enemy of leather, so if you have walked through a peat bog wash your boots thoroughly when you return home. The acid content of whisky-coloured peat water is very high.

Finally, do not leave repairs too long, or the vital leather sub-sole to which a new sole is attached may be damaged. The boots are ready for the repairer when the heel is obviously worn down and the patterned tread of the sole is too shallow to hold small flints.

Treated properly, good-quality boots should have an average life of five to seven years. This can of course be considerably longer or shorter depending on the walker and the terrain covered, but at any rate it should encourage you to go for quality regardless (within reason) of cost.

Clothing

What you wear above your feet is largely a matter of personal choice nowadays. The traditional sail-cloth anorak is still a fairly popular top garment, though it is not nearly as common as it once was. This is largely a result of advances in the design of all-weather overwear, discussed below.

Natural wool shirts and pullovers provide excellent insulation, absorbing sweat without losing warmth. So long as they fit generously, they permit comfortable and easy movement. In colder weather, they should be supplemented with string or thermal vests or a padded waistcoat.

For the lower limbs, jeans are far more popular than they should be. Although they are hard-wearing and fashionable, they are restrictive and, even more important, they provide very poor insulation against cold and wet. Ordinary slacks are far better, preferably twill or a wool and fibre mixture. Genuine walking trousers of Derby tweed or cavalry twill are probably the best for all seasons, save high summer perhaps. Climbing breeches are frequently worn by high-country enthusiasts, but they are not seen very much outside mountain areas.

There is thus a wide choice of general clothing. The only rule–but it is an important one–is that you should wear something reasonably light and non-restrictive that breathes easily and provides efficient insulation.

Wet-weather gear is the exception to this, however. There is nothing more miserable than being wet through, and since any walker in Britain is bound

sooner or later to be exposed to wind and rain it is prudent, to say the least, to protect yourself as well as possible against these unkind elements.

Obviously enough, over-garments must be waterproof. They should also be windproof so that you can maintain body temperature; cut generously to keep condensation to a minimum; and lightweight and unbulky, so that they are easy to carry.

This is asking a great deal. You can for instance stay totally dry in an oilskin suit, but it would be ludicrous to hump such a heavy, bulky item on a long walk. Conversely, you could buy a thin nylon anorak that weighs almost nothing and folds very small. This would be sufficient for high-summer showers, but a great deal of moisture is likely to form under the garment. As in many things, compromise is probably the best policy.

The best over-garments for the top half of the body are made of a substantial nylon material. Although they are reasonably light and acceptably small when folded, they are stout enough to stand up to long-term wear. They give excellent protection against the heaviest and most prolonged rain, and condensation is so minute that it can virtually be ignored. Top over-

The ultimate in self-sufficiency: lightweight materials mean that all this can be carried easily in a single pack.

Latin signs in the lush Sussex countryside remind today's walkers of generations of their predecessors who trod the same paths.

garments should be proofed with several coats of polyurethane, and the seams should be specially treated.

Other features to look out for are:
1 A heavy-duty, two-way zip itself protected by a flap fastened with Velcro. This not only keeps out the wet but also ensures that the garment is totally windproof.
2 Elasticated and adjustable inner cuffs.
3 Spacious pockets specially sewn to prevent water entering.
4 A storm-proof collar.
5 A generously-cut hood with draw-cords for bad weather.

Over-trousers are no less vital than a rain top. However voluminous your raincoat may be, a persistent down-pour will soak both trousers and socks. Quality over-trousers with long side-zips and elasticated waist-bands are easy to slip on or off without removing your boots. Over-trousers may be bought either at the same time as a top or later since, although they are supplied as suits, most retailers sell them separately.

This, then, is the walker's basic outfit, to which must be added maps, compass and—depending on the time of year and the length of the walk—extra clothing, energy-food rations, a first-aid kit and perhaps a camera or binoculars. For anything longer than a day's walk, you will also require overnight things and possibly a brew-up set—that is a stove, canteen, water-bottle and mug and the hot drinks they provide are more than worth the effort of carrying the set.

Rucksacks

If you intend to confine your walking to day-long expeditions, a small, simple rucksack is all you will need, one just large enough for waterproofs, a packed lunch and perhaps a small pullover. Such rucksacks are light and cheap; all equipment shops stock a large number of different models.

Objective walking, which this book hopes to encourage, may entail a hike of anything from two days to two weeks or more, with nights spent at pubs, youth hostels, farmhouses and so on. This requires a rather more spacious rucksack. Backpackers by contrast aim at total self-sufficiency and have to carry a capacious pack. Backpacking may become more appealing as your pedestrian career progresses. It has a very healthy following nowadays, and there are a number of books on it.

The rucksack an objective walker needs is a halfway house between the diminutive day-pack and the big expedition-unit favoured by the back-packer. Good construction and finishing are essential. Try to find a pack made of the relatively new Cordura material; this has the virtues of nylon yet much of the pleasant feel and texture of canvas. The capacity of different models varies, of course. About 30 litres is enough to carry all of life's necessities and a lightweight sleeping bag as well.

Rucksacks must above all be easy to carry. An integral and generously proportioned waist-belt will transfer much of the weight of the pack from the shoulders to the hips. Deep side pockets and external strap-on points are also helpful.

Whichever type of rucksack you choose, take quality into account as well as price. You are after all buying not merely a carrying device but a durable and long-term travelling companion.

One additional hint: no rucksack is totally waterproof, no matter how high its quality. During prolonged storms some water will always seep through the seams and flaps. To keep your possessions tinder dry, use a stout, large plastic bin-liner, which in good weather can double as a groundsheet.

With this compact but comprehensive walking kit, you are equipped to tackle all the footpaths described in this book and to do so with confidence whatever the weather or season of the year. Of course, you will have to find somewhere to stay for the night. This is all part of the fun, and so long as you set off with a reasonably full wallet and a rough idea of your budget there is little risk of being stranded. If you are in doubt ask locally. Someone will always direct you towards a bed and breakfast haven if you are persistent enough.

The Ridgeway Path

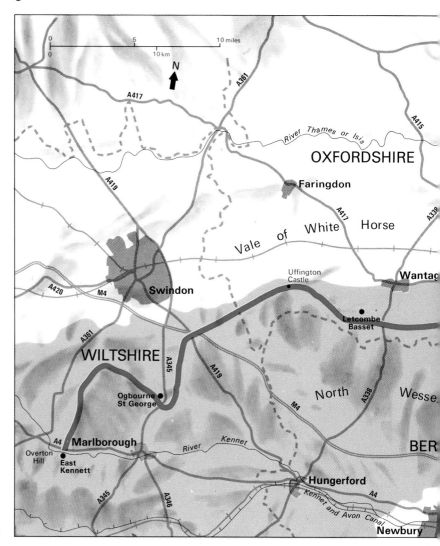

Officially opened 1973
Length: 85 miles
Going: easy

Ordnance Survey maps: 165, 173, 174 and 175

The Ridgeway Path follows the line of the ancient Ridgeway and the Icknield Way along the North Wessex Downs and the Chiltern Hills through five counties of southern England. It offers the walker both a stimulating variety of landscape and a fascinating glimpse into Britain's prehistory.

In many respects, indeed, the Ridgeway is the best route for aspiring distance-walkers wondering where best to open their account. It can be walked in a week and runs through gentle south country that seldom suffers from a severe climate and over terrain that never reaches 1000 feet. Above all, it is superbly defined for almost its entire length. It is the one long-distance path in Britain where map and compass are almost superfluous, especially along the western half, where walkers share an ancient swathe of chalk-down trackway with horse-riders and cyclists.

The modern Ridgeway Path runs over just part of the ancient trackway from which it takes its name. The original route was from the Dorset coast roughly north-east to Stonehenge

and Salisbury Plain, across the Vale of Pewsey and thence along the North Wessex Downs to the Thames at Streatley, where there was probably a ford. The Icknield Way led from Goring, on the opposite bank of the Thames, to Ivinghoe Beacon (the present Path deviates from the original route at times to avoid metalled roads), then on through Bedfordshire and Cambridgeshire to Grimes Graves in west Norfolk and thence to the coast. The wealth of prehistoric sites along these two routes testifies to their significance. Although Avebury (at the western end of the modern Path) and Stonehenge were the most celebrated, and attracted visitors from throughout Britain and abroad, the numerous other barrows, camps and settlements are equal proof that these were major, much trodden pathways.

The Path begins with splendid visual impact at the foot of Overton Hill, west of Marlborough, alongside the A4 and close to Avebury village. Here, at once, the scene is set for many miles to come: voluptuous rounded green hills, part golden with wheat in summer, patchworked by the darker green of tree clumps, and the Path itself, wide and inviting.

Before setting off, the walker would do well to turn aside to visit West Kennett long barrow and the stone circle at Avebury. These will surely catch your imagination, however much you may profess a lack of interest in the past. The long barrow, 330 feet long, 80 feet wide and 10 feet high, was built in about 2500 BC and consists of five stone-lined chambers, in which, over the next millennium, forty-six people were buried. The Bronze Age stone

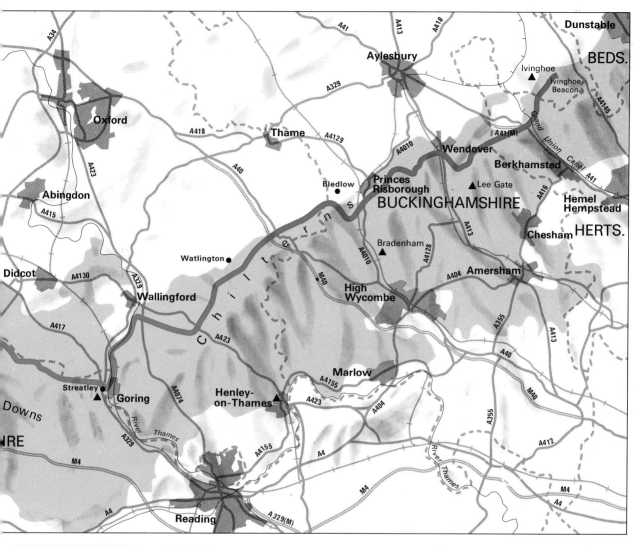

The sarsen stones at the entrance to the West Kennett long barrow, the largest Neolithic chambered tomb in England and Wales and one of the many prehistoric sites at the western end of the Path.

circle at Avebury, less visited and in many ways more impressive than Stonehenge, and more than twelve times as large, was probably a temple: indeed, no other explanation seems possible for so impressive a site.

In the village of Avebury there is an interesting National Trust Museum about the circle and a free car park, although long-term parking may be difficult in high summer. There are several hamlets in the vicinity, however, of which East Kennett is the nearest to the official starting-point of the Path.

East Kennett to Ogbourne 10 miles

The Path marches off across fertile open downs, dotted at first with outlying sarsen stones marking the perimeter of the vast Avebury complex. If the weather is kind this will be a memorable stretch as Overton Hill is climbed and the walker heads towards the high country of Marlborough Downs and the prominent ridge of Hackpen Hill. The Path runs near a nineteenth-century chalk-cut horse (one of several such hill-markers that punctuate the route), but it cannot be seen from the Path itself.

Now the first of many minor roads is crossed, followed by a lofty scarp curving and dipping eastwards, then climbing again to Barbury Castle, a huge Iron Age circular hill-fort. The Path turns southwards now along the fine chalk scarp of Smeathe's Ridge. Below, to the north, is the derelict Ogbourne St George army camp–not quite deserted, in fact, since it is now used as a training ground for urban warfare. On one of the battered house walls some barrack-room wit has scrawled 'You are now entering Free Ogbourne'.

Ogbourne to Letcombe Bassett 18 miles

You enter the huddle of thatched houses that makes up Ogbourne village on a stretch of tarmac, passing a mellow old manor house and church *en route*.

Above right Sarsen stones of the huge 28½-acre Bronze Age Avebury circle, erected in about 1800 BC.

Right The Ridgeway Path as it strides across the Marlborough Downs, a route trodden for thousands of years.

The Path itself skirts the village and then drops to cross the oddly-named river Og in a hamlet called Southend. Here the busy Swindon to Marlborough road is crossed.

Marlborough, with its famous school and elegant main street, lies some 3 miles to the south. There is a first-rate choice of accommodation here and plenty of pubs; the Information Office is housed in the prominent church at the western end of the High Street. Any student of history will enjoy exploring here: it is even claimed that Merlin is buried in the ancient Castle Mound.

Back on the Ridgeway, the bridle-way gradually rises to 600 feet, crossing a couple of lanes and now, in contrast with its previous open aspect, becoming confined between trees and hedges. It is heavy going in places during wet weather and the surface is frequently cut up by horses' hooves, especially on the approach to Round Hill Down.

The Path eventually breaks out into open high country again and traces a route alongside a skein of Iron Age earthworks, barrows and ditches,

Barbury Castle, an Anglo-Saxon hill fort named after Bera, a tribal chief who led his men into battle near here in AD 556.

though their outlines are difficult to trace now. More impressive are the distant views to the north-west, where on a clear day the Cotswold Hills will be clearly etched on the skyline.

Liddington Castle is plain to see on the edge of the scarp, but as at Barbury you will have to make a detour to visit it. The Castle dates from the Iron Age but seems also to have been used until the Anglo-Saxon period. A mile or so of road walking, including a short stretch of the A419, brings you over the M4 and then, at a minor cross-roads a little further on, to the Shepherd's Rest Inn. This may well be a good place to spend a night.

Two grand hills in quick succession, Fox and Charlbury, guarantee to warm up the leg muscles, for here the Path rises to nearly 800 feet as it skirts the village of Bishopstone. The farm country here makes for very pleasant going on the tops, though lanes and roads frequently bisect the Path. Just

Above The celebrated White Horse at Uffington. Various theories have been suggested to explain its origins. It may perhaps have been made in honour of an Iron Age goddess, or it may date from as late as the ninth century AD, cut to record a victorious battle against the Danes.

Right The standing stones guarding Wayland's Smithy, a Stone Age long barrow.

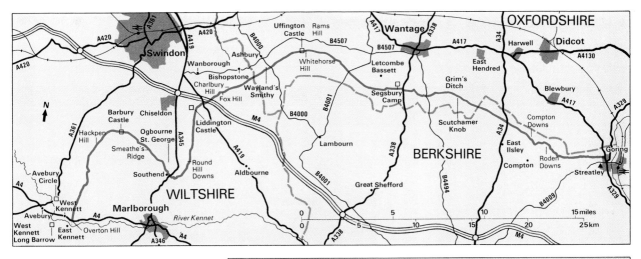

beyond Bishopstone is the Wiltshire/ Oxfordshire boundary, and a couple of miles beyond that you come to one of the prehistoric gems of the whole route, Wayland's Smithy.

The Smithy, a massive chambered long barrow, lies just a short distance off the bridleway within a handsome stand of trees. Legend has it that passing horsemen would leave their mounts (and an appropriate fee) overnight to be shod. In fact the barrow was built in about 2800 BC, some three thousand years before the legend grew up. The ancient tomb is splendidly preserved and is especially magical in the early morning light.

Now the Ridgeway crosses the most dramatic section of the entire route, Uffington Castle and White Horse Hill. As at Wayland's Smithy, you have to turn aside to see the best of this majestic outcrop, but do not hesitate, for the view from the famous elongated White Horse is quite superb. In the immediate foreground is the distinctive Dragon Hill, flat-topped and chalk-scarred, and the Manger, a huge geological gouge in the earth. Beyond, you seem to gaze across half England.

The Uffington earthworks, though evocative enough, are the least impressive of all those along the Ridgeway. The White Horse, however, generally thought to have been cut into the chalk scarp in the first century AD, is a magnificent sight, 365 feet long and 130 feet tall, although never visible in its entirety from ground level.

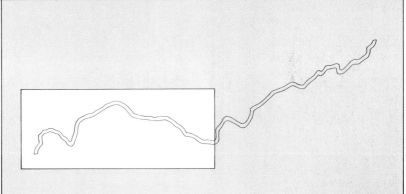

Peaceful Letcombe Bassett, just below the line of the North Wessex Downs, along which the Ridgeway runs.

Back on the wide path, another fine stretch of open country confronts the walker and continues past the summit of Rams Hill, over the B4001, and then high above Letcombe Bassett. The village is picturesque, neatly thatched and devoted to the training of race-horses.

Letcombe Bassett to Streatley
14 miles

Up on the Path, alongside Segsbury Camp, now largely camouflaged by shrubs and trees, a curt farm notice denies walkers access to drinking water. That apart, this is one of the most beautiful sections of the route. A number of horse gallops, wider even than the Ridgeway and used for training race-horses, run parallel to the Path between Letcombe and Lambourn.

The ancient Grim's Ditch joins the Ridgeway where it crosses the B4494 and, though visible for only some of the time, runs with it for some miles. The Ditch was probably built in about the eighth century BC as a boundary-marker between the lands of two neighbouring tribes.

On the skyline are reminders of our own age, Didcot power station and the Atomic Research Establishment at Harwell smudging the view to the north-east. The Path continues wide and green at first, then leads through a wooded swathe to Scutchamer Knob, a Saxon long barrow that marks the county boundary between Oxfordshire and Berkshire.

Some 10 miles of gradual descent follow, passing close to Harwell. The walker's immediate surroundings remain rural, though—arable fields, horse gallops and open sky—even if the hum of urban encroachment does become gradually more noticeable. There are one or two road plods now, and the descent of Crompton Downs is one of the few areas where the Ridgeway is not too well defined. The Path narrows at last after crossing Roden Downs and follows a farm track and then road as it finally dips towards Streatley and the valley of the Thames.

Streatley to Watlington
13 miles

Goring Gap, which separates the Wessex Downs and the Chiltern Hills, marks the halfway point of the walk in more senses than one. From here

Opposite Top The view from White Horse Hill across some of England's most fertile land.

Left Squalls along the Ridgeway near Uffington.

Top The view from below of the Ridgeway, which follows a hilltop route right across southern England.

Above Goring-on-Thames, a popular riverside resort lying in the gap between the North Wessex Downs and the Chiltern Hills.

onwards the Path, with one or two short exceptions, is for walkers only. To a large extent it also heralds the end of those vast plains and open-sky vistas, for after the Thames, with its pretty but meticulously neat weirs below Goring Bridge, the land seems tame by comparison.

From Goring, a friendly little riverside town with a couple of historic pubs, the route follows the towpath at first (the waymarking is a little hazy in parts) through the hamlets of North and South Stoke and then turns abruptly away from the river to round Mongewell Park.

Now, well defined once more, the Path runs due east, mainly along Grim's Ditch again, to the tiny village of Nuffield, where the car magnate and philanthropist William Morris lies buried in the churchyard. A touch of which the great industrialist would surely have approved is a card tacked to the church notice board, telling walkers where to find the water tap.

Watlington is worth a detour, for there is a good choice of accommodation and the mellow town centre is snug and pleasing. There is an excellent pub just half a mile from the Path, The Carriers, justly renowned for its friendly welcome to Ridgeway walkers.

Watlington to Bledlow
8 miles

The going is partly wooded, partly open now, the Path once more wide and easy as it runs well below the summit of Watlington Hill and the succeeding heights of Pyrton, Shirburn and Bald. Shirburn, by the way, at 835 feet is the highest in Oxfordshire. The Path now ducks under the M40, then skirts Beacon Hill above Lewknor village and continues along the Icknield Way over the busy A40. The going is pleasant enough despite this sudden excess of roads and traffic.

On the approach to Chinnor, there is a huge cement works and much quarrying around it. One might think that with roads and clattering industry this stretch would not be among the best the Ridgeway has to offer. Curiously, though, the walker somehow remains detached, the natural beauty of Bledlow Great Wood drawing the eye and the Path beckoning towards Ledge Hill above Bledlow, then providing fine views over Princes Risborough.

Bledlow to Wendover
10 miles

The descent into Princes Risborough has one or two overgrown sections, and there are two railway crossings to be made and a length of road-walking. The old part of the town has a number of pleasant buildings, but there is a sizeable ring of modern housing on the outskirts. The Path rounds the town to the south and veers east away from the Icknield Way to climb Whiteleaf Hill, continuing along the lower slopes of Pulpit Hill.

A downhill dog-leg follows as the Ridgeway actually passes through Chequers, the gracious rural seat of the nation's prime ministers. There can be few countries in the world where foot-travellers may approach so close to the residence of the national leader: a moment to savour our democratic heritage. Gaps in the parkland trees

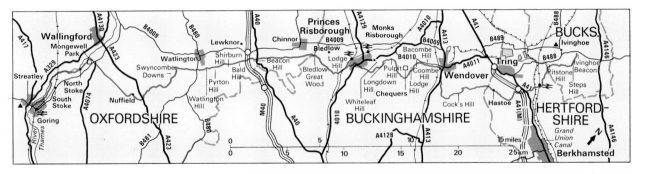

Left Beacon Hill between Princes Risborough and Wendover. According to legend King Cymbeline – the ancient British monarch of whom Shakespeare wrote – had a palace near here.

Above Chequers, the country home of the nation's prime ministers. Walkers may follow the Path unmolested through the grounds.

Right Cottages at Wendover, a pleasant
country town astride the Path.

Below Ivinghoe Beacon, the highest point in
the Chilterns, marks the end of the
Ridgeway Path.

provide tantalising glimpses of the magnificent sixteenth-century mansion.

It is fine wooded country now, with near-aerial views, as you ascend and cross three hills in quick succession, Lodge, Coombe and Bacombe. A needle monument on top of Coombe Hill pinpoints the highest viewpoint along the Chilterns, just over 850 feet. The subsequent descent to Wendover, where a number of pubs are waiting, is an easy delight.

Wendover to Ivinghoe Beacon
12 miles

From here the Ridgeway describes a wide southerly sweep, as if reluctant to complete the final stretch. You can cheat a little by walking along roads at first east of Wendover, but purists will stay with the path from Wellhead Inn across Cock's Hill. There is a section of urban road-walking east of Hastoe hamlet as you zig-zag around Tring via lanes and minor roads, crossing an old Roman road (disguised now as the A41), the Grand Union Canal and the railway line.

Now your spirits must rise as surely as your elevation as you stride northwards over Pitstone Hill past the splendidly restored seventeenth-century windmill and on again to the lofty finale. Gradually, above Ivinghoe, the scene becomes more and more dramatic, culminating in true splendour atop the renowned Ivinghoe Beacon.

The windmill on Pitstone Hill, one of the last ascents the walker on the Ridgeway Path must tackle.

The South Downs Way

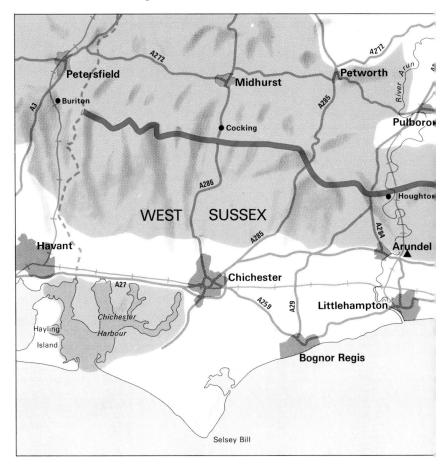

Officially opened 1972
Length: 80 miles
Going: easy

Ordnance Survey maps: 197, 198 and 199

There are a number of reasons why the South Downs Way, which follows the ridge of the South Downs across Sussex from Eastbourne in the east to the Hampshire border in the west, is one of the most popular long-distance paths. First and foremost, it is easy walking, and so long as you have made some effort to get into shape you should not find it at all difficult. It runs through gentle country, and although it keeps to a high level its comparatively modest altitude rules out any threat of exposure. Indeed, the path may be tackled safely at almost any time of the year.

The Way is also very well defined, especially at the eastern end, which is the usual–and most spectacular–starting-point. Since it follows the rim of an escarpment that is always within easy reach of civilization, it presents few if any navigation problems, and there is absolutely no chance of getting lost. But although the path passes near some of the busiest parts of southern England, you should not think of it as some kind of urban park: there are places, barely more than a stone's

throw from Brighton, where the walker might imagine himself in the Derbyshire Peak District.

Before you set off, however, a word of caution against over-confidence is in order. Easy the path may be, but this does not mean you can dispense with map and compass. And wear stout boots, whatever the season. The surface of the path is frequently a blend of flint and chalk which, although firm, can be tiring if you are wearing flimsy footwear. In addition, heavy rain regularly makes a number of spots along the Way practically impassable for mud.

Eastbourne to Alfriston
11 miles

If you arrive at the celebrated starting-point by car, look for a car-park in Eastbourne. To leave it at Beachy Head is not only tempting fate but is unsociable, for space is limited. In any case this is an out-of-court practice since the path actually begins in the town.

There are two routes to begin with, the bridleway, which turns inland

immediately, and the footpath, which winds steeply upwards to Beachy Head. The footpath is of course the most dramatic and is preferred by most walkers. It must be said, however, that one of the finest views of the whole South Downs Way is to be had from the bridleway at Windover Hill; in addition, the inland path does pass close to the Long Man of Wilmington, of whom more in a moment.

The footpath starts with a short sharp climb of some 500 feet from the promenade at the western end of the town. As you gain the top of Beachy Head you will surely look back more than once at the genteel resort spread out below you. The path is tarmac for a short time as it approaches the signal station, now, like Belle Tout lighthouse, disused, but soon it crosses springy turf, the best surface for the start of a walk.

Past Birling Gap (once a favourite spot for landing contraband), the path follows the unmade road beside the hotel back on to the cliff tops. The next few miles are a magnificent roller-

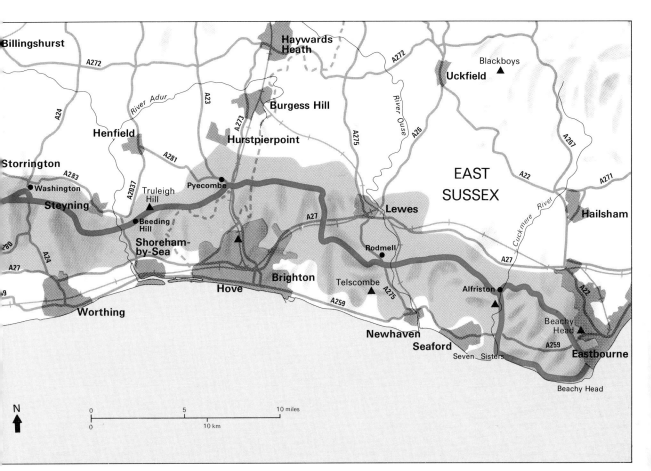

Beachy Head lighthouse, whose beam can be seen 16 miles into the Channel. The lighthouse was built in 1902 to replace the Belle Tout light, which the South Downs Way passes on the cliffs above.

The Seven Sisters seen from Birling Gap, an exhilarating prelude–or conclusion–to the 80-mile downland route.

coaster over the famous Seven Sisters (there are eight of them in fact). Pause to enjoy the fine seascapes, for the Way never again comes so close to the English Channel. After Haven Brow, the last Sister, a steepish chalk track descends to Cuckmere Haven, from where the path takes you along the river bank, across the busy A259 coast road and into Friston Forest.

More downhill walking brings you now to the hamlet of Westdean. From here forest rides and a quiet road lead through a wooded valley to Litlington (where they claim to have the smallest church in England, although Culbone near Porlock on the South-West Peninsula Coast Path would surely dispute this) and on to Alfriston.

Just before the village, at Plonk Barn, the footpath and the bridleway converge. For the remaining 70-odd miles, walkers will find themselves sharing their route with cyclists and

horse-riders, for the Way is in fact a long-distance bridleway, the first to be so designated. Alfriston itself has accommodation, picturesque pubs and a fine old church, known locally as the Cathedral of the Downs.

Even though it means making a short detour, follow the bridleway eastwards to Wilmington Hill and the famous Long Man of Wilmington, a mysterious chalk-cut figure with a staff in each hand, standing some 240 feet high. Those who have followed the bridleway all the way from Eastbourne will of

Above The cross at Alfriston. The inn name behind recalls what was once one of the village's main pursuits.

Right The Long Man of Wilmington. One belief has it that the figure is King Harold, last of the Saxon kings of England.

course see him anyway. Below, in the village, the remains of a fourteenth-century Benedictine priory are well worth a visit.

Alfriston to Newmarket Inn
15 miles

From Alfriston the path, now chalk and flint, gradually ascends to Firle Beacon, which, at an elevation of 713 feet, provides another fine view. Next there is a gradual descent to the valley of the river Ouse and, after the road, railway and river have been crossed in quick succession, to Southease, a pretty little hamlet astride the path. A short stretch of road walking brings you to Rodmell, where the Abergavenny Arms is a popular pub among South Downs walkers.

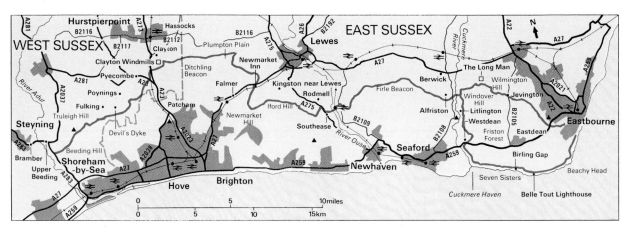

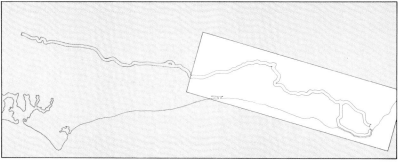

A steady ascent follows, steep at first, along the tops to Newmarket Hill. Just past Iford Hill, a path branches off to the village of Kingston near Lewes, one of a number of local tracks. The Way dog-legs west and north alongside woods and then dips to pass beneath the railway before reaching the A27 and another well-placed pub, the Newmarket Inn.

Just a couple of miles off the Way, Lewes is a popular halt, with plenty of accommodation available. There has been a settlement here since Saxon times, and the castle dominates the narrow streets and attractive buildings of the town. The two museums owned by the Sussex Archaeological Society are well worth seeing.

Newmarket Inn to Pyecombe
9 miles

From here there is more woodland walking at first through a number of plantations, with the 800-foot Ditchling Beacon the distant objective. You climb northwards to Plumpton Plain, then west for a straight and steady course first to the Beacon and then on towards Clayton Windmills, nick-named Jack and Jill, making another dog-leg just before you reach them. Now comes the descent to Pyecombe, where you are roughly one third of the way along the path. There is a youth hostel at Patcham alongside the A23 road to Brighton and camping at the Brighton municipal site in Sheepcote Valley, a couple of miles east of the town. Pyecombe itself has an old forge, where shepherds' crooks were once made. Brighton, of course, scarcely needs any recommendation, with its extraordinary, luxurious Pavilion, excellent museum and multitude of fascinating shops.

Walkers on the Way near Lewes, a classic scene of open vistas and rolling downland.

Left Riders near Clayton. Unlike most other long-distance paths, the South Downs Way is a bridleway and thus open to horse-riders and cyclists as well as to walkers.

Pyecombe to Upper Beeding
8 miles

As you leave Pyecombe and approach Devil's Dyke, the view westwards towards Chanctonbury Ring is magnificent. The Dyke is a splendid downland combe, and the path provides commanding views over the low-lying Sussex hinterland. This is a very popular area with day visitors based at Brighton, and the Way is crossed by a number of paths and roads. The clutter soon gives way to pleasant walking over a fairly well defined route to Truleigh Hill, where there is a transmitter station and a youth hostel. Rather more than a mile later you come to a footpath junction at Beeding Hill, where the Society of Sussex Downsmen erected a signpost to commemorate their Diamond Jubilee in 1973.

Left The view from Ditchling Beacon. In the best weathers, the panorama extends as far as the North Downs, some 30 miles to the north.

Top Bramber, once one of William the Conqueror's provincial capitals and a busy port.

Above Devil's Dyke, said to have been part of a ditch dug by the devil inland from the Channel to destroy the churches of the Weald. Disturbed by a woman carrying a light, the devil fled, leaving his work unfinished.

Upper Beeding to Houghton
15 miles

The Way crosses the river Adur, and riverside paths lead north to Bramber and Upper Beeding. There is more escarpment walking now alongside the rim of Annington Hill and then some farmland stretches, a length of metalled road and, finally, above Wiston Park, a footpath again to bring you to Chanctonbury Ring. The Ring itself is a prehistoric earthwork, but the distinctive clump of trees was not planted until the eighteenth century.

A wide, well-used flint track drops to the A24, where there is a choice of two routes from the busy main road to Chantry Hill. There are good views again from here. Some ups and downs follow before the summit of Amberley Mount above the Arun valley is reached and the path descends to the river. Arundel and its magnificent castle some three miles to the south make a worthwhile diversion from here, and there is also a youth hostel in the town.

Houghton to Cocking
11 miles

There is interesting history close to the path as you climb again from the river through Houghton and over Bury and Westburton Hills to the heights above Bignor. In the village, 2½ miles away, the Roman villa has some well-preserved mosaic floors. We also cross Stane Street here, built ruler-straight inland from Chichester to London in the early years of the Roman occupation of Britain.

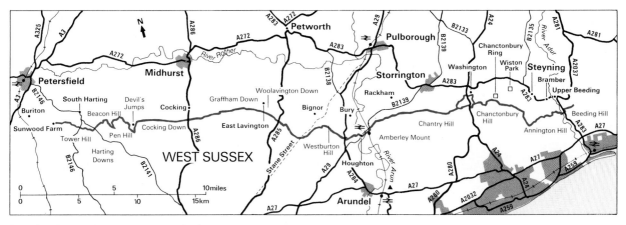

Opposite The beech wood on the summit of Chanctonbury Ring, still a mysterious place, especially in winter, when the crowds have vanished.

Opposite below The river Arun from the bridge at Houghton on the South Downs Way.

Below Arundel castle, a few miles south of the Way. Norman in origin, the castle – home of the Duke of Norfolk, Earl Marshal of England – was rebuilt in the eighteenth century and restored in 1890.

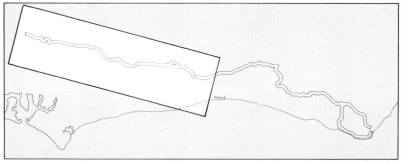

Above Medieval yeoman's cottage at Bignor, north of the path. Here there is also a Roman villa with fine mosaic floors.

The countryside becomes more wooded now, and there is a spate of green hills all about 800 feet high, some of the highest in fact along the South Downs. North of here lies Midhurst, still a charming country town, and Cowdray Park, renowned for its polo matches. Sporting enthusiasts might turn south, to Goodwood race-course, and history-lovers will want to visit the Weald and Downland Open Air Museum at Singleton, a mile or so south on the A286, where there is a magnificent collection of historic farm and village buildings.

Cocking to Buriton
11 miles

On the western side of the A286 Cocking Down is a particularly good viewpoint. From here you can see the spire of Chichester cathedral and part of the huge natural harbour. A mile or so further on, half-hidden just to the right of the path, are the Devil's Jumps, an intriguing line of Bronze Age burial mounds. The path now continues through pleasant woodland, then climbs to the top of Pen Hill, swoops steeply down to Millpond Bottom and winds around Beacon Hill.

After crossing the B2141 and the B2146, the Way follows Forty Acre Lane for a couple of miles to the Hampshire border just short of Sunwood Farm. Although the Way officially ends here, Buriton village, reached via Cockshott Wood and a cart track to the parish church, is the more sensible finishing-post. Here, some two miles south of Petersfield, is a charming little village, an apt conclusion to the walk, with the Maple Inn ready to provide refreshment and accommodation.

Above Winter view of Linch Down, a few miles from the western end of the Way.

Left The church and pond at Buriton, near Petersfield. For the moment the village marks the finish of the Way, although suggestions for an extension west to Winchester have been made.

The North Downs Way

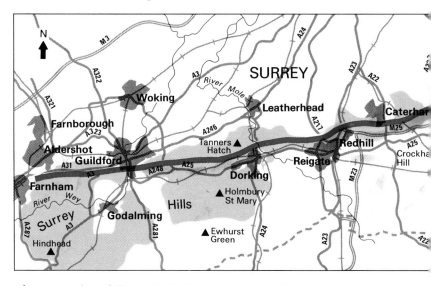

Officially opened 1978

Length: 140 miles, including the Canterbury loop

Going: easy

Ordnance Survey maps: 178, 179, 186, 187, 188 and 189

In parts, the North Downs Way, which runs virtually the whole length of the North Downs, from Farnham in west Surrey to Dover in south-east Kent, is more frequently trodden than any other long-distance path in the country. And yet, paradoxically, it is probably the route least walked in its entirety.

There are many reasons why this is so. The Way's proximity to London and the southern suburbs, and also to the Medway conurbation, makes it ideal for day and weekend outings. However, some very pretty country and one or two memorable high stretches notwithstanding, as a whole the path is less than satisfactory. Route-finding is very frustrating in places: there is a fair amount of little-used, overgrown pathway that only diligent map-readers will be able to navigate; and, by way of equally unwelcome contrast, a good deal of walking on metalled roads is required. It must be admitted too that there is little of the deeply rewarding continuity

of routes such as Offa's Dyke Path or the Pennine Way and only a limited amount of their greatest asset, genuine open countryside.

If the landscape is not all that might be desired, the North Downs Way has much to offer historically. In places it coincides with the Pilgrims' Way, the route (much of it now covered by metalled road) taken by medieval pilgrims travelling from Winchester to Canterbury. The path itself is older still and has been trodden since prehistoric times. In addition, it takes the walker through a panorama of British history: near prehistoric earthworks and Roman sites, through unspoilt medieval villages and handsome Georgian towns, to Canterbury, mother church of the worldwide Anglican community and scene of the murder of Thomas à Becket, and on to the symbolic and celebrated White Cliffs of Dover.

Farnham to Guildford
12 miles

The Way begins in the valley of the river Mole alongside the buzzing A31 road just south of Farnham. There is towpath walking at first, close to the old Georgian town centre, once one of the biggest grain markets in England. Past Farnham Golf Course the path rises steadily to wind round Crooksbury Hill, near Seale village and over Puttenham Common.

Ironically, the best views from the aptly-named Hog's Back are denied the walker, for the crest is occupied by the A31. The path below the southern ridge is pleasant enough, however, and

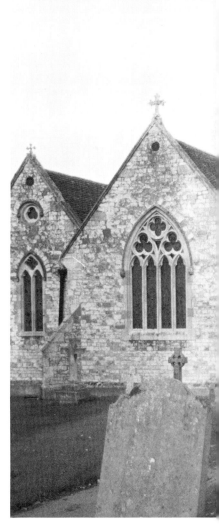

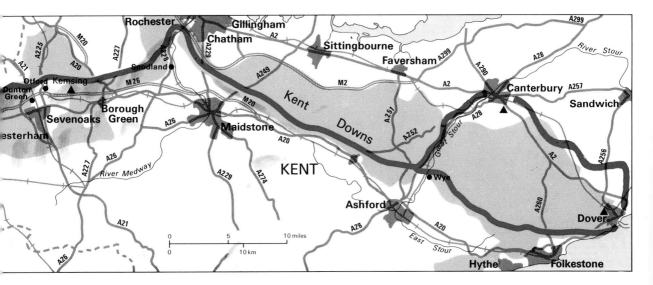

The church at Seale, at the western end of the Hog's Back, and a few miles from the start of the Way in Farnham.

Right The seventeenth-century Guildhall at Guildford. An astonishing range of architecture awaits the visitor here, including a Norman keep, the sixteenth-century grammar school and seventeenth-century almshouses. The mid-twentieth century cathedral stands prominent on Stag Hill, and, immediately below it, the even more recent buildings of the university.

Stepping-stones across the river Mole near Dorking, one of the stretches along which the newly created North Downs Way and the ancient Pilgrims' Way coincide.

at Puttenham the Jolly Farmers Inn is a favourite half-way house. From here the path follows a well-defined track, some of it wooded, to an arched passage under the A3. It is largely road walking through Compton and then along the Pilgrims' Way south of Guildford and the river Wey, which is usually crossed either in the town or at a lock about half a mile to the south. A footbridge on the path itself is promised. Guildford, first of the three cathedral cities on the North Downs Way, is well worth exploring, if only for the picturesque cobbled high street and the fine old Guildhall.

Guildford to Dorking
14 miles

The path forsakes the Pilgrims' Way now for more scenic surroundings and climbs Albury Downs, giving wide views from Newlands Corner, a popular picnic spot and best avoided at summer weekends. There is more pleasant going now along a bridleway and a minor road through pretty woods and then across Netley Heath.

The route continues over Ranmore Common, through the Denbies estate (now owned by the National Trust) and thence to the lower ground by the river Mole. The busy A24 and the diminutive river are negotiated by underpass and stepping-stones respectively.

**Dorking to Merstham
13 miles**

Outstanding landscapes may be few and far between on the Way, but the next stretch, from Box Hill to Reigate,

is as impressive and beautiful a high-level route as any in southern England. It is also thronged by hosts of strollers and car picnickers at weekends. If you tackle this stretch on a weekday or outside high summer, however, you will see it much as it was in the days of Keats and Nelson, both of whom loved the area.

Route-finding can be a little confusing around here. Ignore the mass of criss-cross paths and keep steadily on an eastward course across Brockham and Betchworth Hills. Here the

The view westwards from Box Hill. One of the best-known beauty spots in southern England, the Hill is crowded with visitors in summer; at other seasons there are only walkers to enjoy its peace.

43

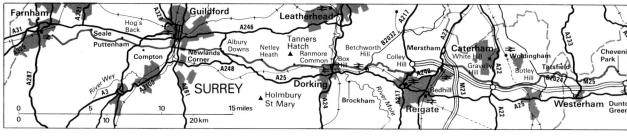

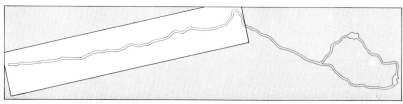

Below Box Hill, one of the highlights of the Way. The seventeenth-century diarist John Evelyn wrote of the Hill that the evergreens made it seem 'summer all the winter'.

landscape is patched with thick woods, mostly of box trees, from which, of course, Box Hill gets its name.

Eventually the path descends to cross Pebble Hill Road and then ascends to Colley Hill, one of the most dramatic and attractive scarps along the Way. There are wide panoramas over Reigate and beyond from here and numerous chalk pits excavated in the surprisingly steep hillsides. The going is heavy in some places, especially in wet weather, but the path is well defined as it reaches the summit of Colley Hill and pushes on across Reigate Hill. While the Way is pleasant enough near Gatton Park, the scene changes as the walker nears Merstham, with uniform housing developments and a skein of busy roads.

Merstham to Otford
18 miles

At Merstham you negotiate the M25 by a footbridge and the M23 by an under-pass, after which there is no alternative to walking along the A23 for a short stretch. Now the Way climbs White Hill and Gravelly Hill and reaches the A22, which is spanned by a footbridge. Four major roads in quick succession make this a section most people are thankful to leave behind. Even here there are compensations, however, with frequent green wooded pockets, Arthur's Seat, an outcrop on White Hill and once a prehistoric settlement, and finally the view from the top of Gravelly Hill.

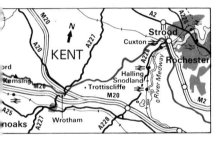

Right The statue of Sir Winston Churchill on Westerham Green, a few miles south of the Way. Chartwell, Churchill's country home, lies a little further south.

The path runs south of Woldingham village and then along a pleasant high-level track over Botley Hill to the Surrey/Kent border at Tatsfield. The village, a little to the north of the path, is a favourite overnight stopping-place. Alternatively, you could press on to Westerham, a finely preserved old market town.

The route now becomes more rural again as it penetrates further into the Kentish Weald. Route-finding is easier, too, as there are more signposts,

each displaying the distinctive acorn symbol. There is pleasant walking over the contoured countryside around Chevening Park, and then the path descends once more to the valley floor to Dunton Green, where the A21 is crossed, and, on the other side of the Darent valley, to the ancient village of Otford. The evocative remains of an old Palace of the Archbishops of Canterbury, rebuilt in 1501, can still be seen, and there is also a Roman villa nearby at Lullingstone.

Otford Church with its striking twelfth-century tower. Much of the stonework in the nave dates from the Norman Conquest.

Otford to Rochester
15 miles

Outside Otford the path climbs again to the rim of the Downs, hugging a wooded scarp past Hildenborough Hall. Further on, at Wrotham, it crosses the busy A20 London to Folkestone road. It is worth pausing a while here, for Wrotham is a mellow, largely unspoiled village with a long history and an interesting old church.

Splendid views ahead over the Weald and the Medway valley signal a subtle change in both terrain and atmosphere, as the cosy Surrey countryside gives way to the wider, brisker land of Kent; here already there is a faint scent of salt breezes. Above Trottiscliffe the path follows the Pilgrims' Way. On the outskirts of Rochester, however, the green and pleasant backwater terminates temporarily, and the wide and often swift Medway is crossed by the footpath alongside the M2.

Rochester to Charing
13 miles

No doubt relieved to escape the unending stream of traffic spilling across the bridge, the walker follows the path as it veers away from the motorway and ascends to the tranquility of Wouldham Downs and Bluebell Hill. The route is not well defined at this point, and careful map-reading between here and Detling will probably be necessary to avoid trespassing. From Detling the path runs more or less parallel to the

Above The North Downs Way near Trottiscliffe. Here the walker treads in the footsteps of generations of medieval pilgrims making their way to Thomas à Becket's shrine in Canterbury cathedral.

Opposite Kentish farmland in the Medway valley. Such fine, wide landscapes are ever present in the Kentish sections of the Way.

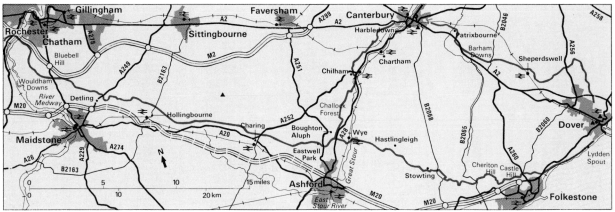

Pilgrims' Way to Hollingbourne, where the two join and continue to Charing.

Charing is the gateway to the orchard country of Kent and remains a delightful village despite the modern development surrounding it. The Archbishop of Canterbury once had a palace here, and there are a number of eighteenth-century timbered houses in the main street and a delightful square. Despite the nearby main road, the village manages to retain an air of timeless tranquility.

Charing to Wye
10 miles

At this point comes the second wide break in the line of the Downs, the Great Stour gap, and the path from Charing gradually descends to the river valley via footways and quiet lanes through apple orchards. Wye is another delightful village. There is an immaculately preserved centre, with a number of interesting old houses, some half-timbered, and a renowned agricultural college.

Wye to Canterbury
12 miles

Shortly before Wye, at Boughton Lees, the path divides. The northern route follows the Pilgrims' Way to Canterbury via Challock Forest and Chilham, proclaimed one of the prettiest villages in England. Its famous castle has a Norman keep and seventeenth-century additions, built on Roman foundations.

A splendid stretch brings the walker over high ridge hills and through woodland to Chartham Hatch and then across farm and orchard country to Harbledown. And so at last the great walled cathedral city is reached, which the long-distance walker may enter for

Below The path between Hollingbourne and Detling, one of the finest stretches along the ridge of the Downs.

Right The square at Chilham. The timbered houses are Tudor, and the church dates from the fifteenth century.

Below right The tower of Charing church. The legend on the sundial reads 'Life's but a shadow, redeem the time'.

Right Canterbury cathedral, among the finest ecclesiastical buildings in the land. This was the end of the road for medieval pilgrims; today's walkers have another 15 miles to Dover before them.

Below The view towards Shakespeare Cliff, Dover, the end (and the beginning) of the Way.

all the world like a pilgrim of old. There is a youth hostel here and a camping-ground on the Sandwich road. At least a day will be needed to visit the cathedral, the monastic buildings, St Augustine's Abbey and the Roman remains.

Canterbury to Dover
15 miles

From Canterbury the loop route continues eastwards through unspoiled orchard country to Patrixbourne and then over Barham Downs: here one

realizes why Kent is described as the Garden of England. The path dog-legs from Shepherdswell and then follows the old Roman road south into Dover.

Wye to Dover
18 miles

The shorter, direct route from Wye to Dover begins by climbing from the Great Stour valley to the ridge of Downs above Hastingleigh and then drops down to Stowting village. Now the five impressive hills surrounding Folkestone–Cheriton, Cherry Garden,

Castle, Round and Sugar Loaf–are crossed, and the path joins the A260 high above the town centre at the Valiant Sailor pub.

The final stretch is along the famous White Cliffs. There are excellent views of the English Channel, and on fine days France stands out clean and clear. If the army ranges are active at Lydden Spout, a short road detour will be necessary. Otherwise, it will be a dramatic finish at Shakespeare Cliff above the bustling port and almost in the shadow of the castle.

Wye Downs, one of the most impressive moments on the direct route between Wye and Dover.

Offa's Dyke Path

Officially opened 1971
Length: 168 miles
Going: hard

Ordnance Survey maps: 116, 117, 126, 137, 148, 161 and 162

Offa's Dyke Path, the only coast-to-coast long-distance route in the country, runs the entire length of the border between England and Wales. It takes the walker through scenery more varied than that offered by any other long-distance route: the pastoral lowlands of the Severn valley, thick woodlands in the Wye valley and the stern, sometimes savage, uplands in the Black Mountains and the Clwydian Hills. Despite its name, the Path has been planned to follow quiet and beautiful border country rather than stay with the line of the ancient Dyke regardless.

The official starting-point, on Sedbury Cliffs, on the western bank of the Severn estuary, is something of a disappointment. True, there is a massive, though largely overgrown, section of the Dyke. But the Path is soon obliterated and becomes difficult to trace.

Much the better and more convenient departure point is Chepstow. There is a camping site at the Racecourse and a youth hostel just south-west of the town centre. Before

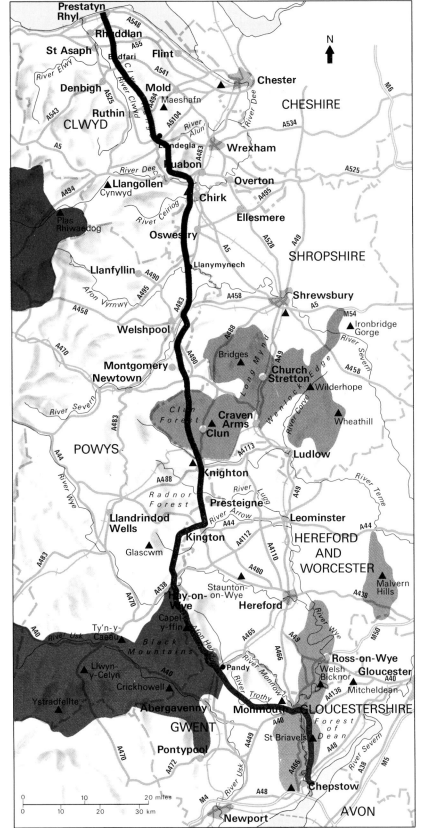

The fortifications at Chepstow, the first Norman castle built in Wales. The stronghold straddles the route west from England and also overlooks the harbour. Today the town is the best departure point for walkers tackling Offa's Dyke Path from south to north.

you lock the car and set off, though, do drive across the magnificent Severn Toll Bridge. In the centre of the great span, glance to the north-east, for there, stretching invitingly into the distance, lies the route of the Path.

Chepstow to Monmouth
16 miles

Chepstow itself is well worth a brief visit. The impressive castle, whose walls rise sheer from the river, was begun by the Normans and finished during the thirteenth century to defend a strategic bend in the river Wye. Just walking around and looking at the mellow old buildings will give you a sense of this town's long history.

From the town centre a link footpath crosses the Wye and almost immediately joins the main Path. A short, steep climb takes you past the growth area of Tutshill, and then almost immediately you are tramping alongside the Dyke itself, the first of many brief flirtations with Offa's legacy. And now that you are gaining both altitude and rural peace, not to mention some splendid views as you approach Tintern Abbey, some words about the history of the Dyke and its builder will not be out of place.

Offa was king of Mercia (very roughly central and southern England

with the addition, towards the end of his reign, of East Anglia) from 757 to 796 and was the most powerful of all the Anglo-Saxon monarchs. Work on the Dyke did not begin until 784, and it is almost certain that it was intended to mark an agreed, definite frontier between Mercia and the various Welsh kingdoms to the west. The border had fluctuated for hundreds of years, and it was only in about 780, after a last Welsh attack, that relative peace was achieved.

The Dyke, then, was primarily a frontier-marker. It also enabled trade to be controlled, as traffic could only pass through fixed gaps in it, and it may also have prevented, or at the very least hindered, cattle raids.

Each landowner along the route of the Dyke was responsible for construction work on his section, and to some extent this may account for the variations in construction and scale. On the whole, however, the earth bank of the Dyke was 6 feet high and some 60 feet wide; it was always ditched, usually on the west side, sometimes on both.

About 81 miles of earthworks can be traced today, and there is one unbroken stretch of 60 miles–from Kington to Chirk–where the long-distance path follows the Dyke more or less continuously. The modern walker

Top Tintern Abbey, set in a curve of the river Wye. The Abbey was founded in 1131, rebuilt a century and a half later and suppressed in 1536.

Above The market at Monmouth, the last major town on Offa's Dyke Path for many miles. The town dates from Roman times and was an important frontier settlement during the Middle Ages.

can only marvel at the back-breaking work that must have been involved, especially along those high, stern stretches that remain untamed today.

At the southern end of the Path, however, there is only a hint of the tough and exciting terrain to come as progress is made along the lush Wye valley. There are high spots such as Wintours Leap above Broadbrook, but in the main this is deeply wooded, rounded-contour country, skirting the green Forest of Dean. The Path, well walked and therefore well defined, follows the river and one or two short sections of the Dyke and gives a fine elevated view from the Devil's Pulpit across the river to Tintern Abbey. There is a short detour path down to this curiously magnetic shell of stone, timeless and evocative, a place of worship since the thirteenth century.

Two routes run roughly parallel from Tintern towards St Briavels. The towpath is easier than the hill path and provides a pleasant waterside walk as far as Bigsweir Bridge. There is a youth hostel about 1½ miles from here at St Briavels and many of the riverside farms permit camping. There is limited accommodation too at Lower Redbrook, where the Path briefly meets the road. You may well wish to call it a day hereabouts, leaving the strenuous stretch over Kymin Hill and into Monmouth until tomorrow.

Crossing Kymin Hill you pass the Naval Temple built to commemorate a number of late eighteenth-century admirals. There is something distinctly pleasing about marching down once more to the river and this fine old town. Here there is a museum devoted to Lord Nelson, statues of Henry V (who

was born in the castle) and Charles Rolls, of Rolls-Royce fame, and the Georgian Shire Hall is a particularly fine building. This is the last town of any size actually astride the Path until Prestatyn, at the very end, and the foot traveller may well feel like pausing before heading towards the Black Mountains and to some of the least populated high country in Great Britain.

Monmouth to Pandy
16 miles

The contrast in the country is not immediately apparent as you dog-leg south then west through Monmouth after crossing the famous thirteenth-century fortified bridge over the river Monnow. There is road walking at first, then pleasant, if unspectacular, low-level going largely over river pasture and rich farming country.

Distant view of the Black Mountains, where the walker encounters some of the toughest stretches on the entire Path.

The route takes you on a gradual climb over track and road towards the Black Mountains, past the distinctive pub at Llantilio-Crossenny where there has been an inn since the fifteenth century. Then path and road bring you to White Castle, a squat, round-towered ruin and border stronghold dating from the twelfth century. There is a youth hostel not too far from here, at Capel-y-Ffin.

Another very old (and welcome) pub greets you after an undulating, muscle-stretching section. The Hunters Moon Inn at Llangattock was built in the seventeenth century and remains largely unchanged. Take a longish rest here, for ahead lies the majestic

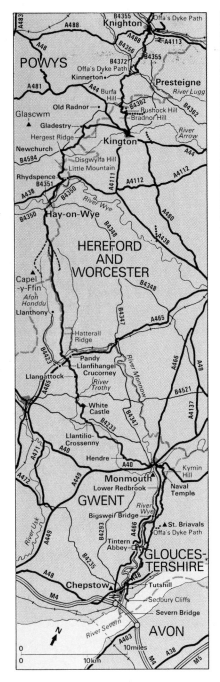

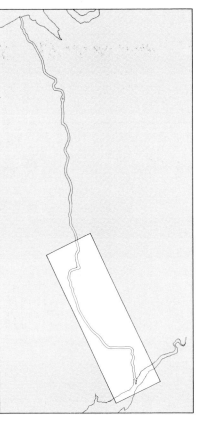

Above centre The river Wye and the Black Mountains near Hay-on-Wye in winter.

Right The walker's view from the Path above Hay.

level route. Here you are in the Black Mountains and they do not come by their name lightly.

Indeed, it is another world along the Ridge, seemingly untrodden, with a great plateau of coarse grass, heather and the occasional Iron Age barrow, your only company sheep and ponies. The views are wide and splendid, the going hard, even gruelling in places, particularly after rainy spells. Even the most energetic usually opt for the descent to Llanthony, where there is a pub, a camping-ground and an old Priory, despite the hard slog needed to regain the tops.

There is more rough going from here, decidedly switchback and tough on the muscles, and under cloud or mist it seems black and forbidding in the extreme, especially from the summit of Hay Bluff. The panoramic views from here on a fine day, though, are absolutely magnificent. You may well have to refer to map and compass frequently on this last stretch before dropping down the scarp to Hay, for there are some confusing lateral footpaths and the way-marking is none too clear.

Eventually you come down to a less hostile elevation to join the skein of farm tracks and lanes that mean the end of moorland walking for a while and with Hay-on-Wye no doubt by now an eager objective. You will have no sterner walk than this anywhere along the route. Some award that accolade to the next stretch, however, so there is no cause to feel too complacent.

Hay is an old-world town, nestling under the northern scarp of the Black Mountains. It was once a border fortress settlement as the remains of two Norman castles testify. All the creature comforts the foot traveller needs are here, plus a choice of accommodation. Shop opening times are a shade erratic, perhaps proof of the inhabitants' independence of mind.

Hatterrall Ridge, almost awesome when first sighted from low level and one of the finest mountain-top routes on the entire Dyke Path. Suddenly, emerging from the patchwork Monmouth lowlands, you are faced with a wild sky-scraping path that in places reaches 2,000 feet and more. Just off the Path and conveniently located as a rest area before you tackle the ascent are Pandy and Llanfihangel-Crucorney. There is a good choice of accommodation here, including a camping-ground, and, among other buildings of interest, an old pub where the notorious Judge Jeffreys used to dispense law, if not justice.

Pandy to Hay-on-Wye
17 miles

Given just a touch of luck with the weather, the next few miles should be among the most memorable of the walk. But it should also be emphasized that the Ridge is a high and very lonely place, especially above Llanthony, and if bad weather is obviously brewing even the most experienced walkers should wait or avoid the wildest summits by taking the alternative low-

Hay-on-Wye to Kington
15 miles

From Hay the Path takes you through pastures and lanes at first. Then, inevitably, the land begins to rise as you follow the old Hereford county line and cross the A4153. Most walkers find their way to the picturesque Rhydspence Inn before taking to lanes and tracks to rejoin the main footpath near the site of a Roman camp on Little Mountain. From the tiny hamlet of

Above Hay-on-Wye, staging-post on Offa's Dyke Path and end point of the 36-mile Wye Valley Walk (see page 148) upstream to Rhayader. The town is also a magnet for bibliophiles, possessing an astonishing number of second-hand bookshops.

Right Lush country near Hay, typical of the lower-level sections of the Path.

Newchurch the Path strikes out across Disgwylfa Hill and then down into Gladestry, another hamlet with a pub and a shop.

It is fine walking now with some splendid views as you negotiate green tracks to the height of Hergest Ridge. If the weather is kind your horizon may be 30 miles away up here and you will be almost reluctant to make the gradual descent from the 1300-foot summit into Kington. Your leg muscles, on the other hand, may well appreciate the rest.

Kington, a smallish town bisected by the A44, is located on the banks of the river Arrow, where, once again, there has been a settlement since Norman times. Little remains of those early days, but from the practical angle the town is a welcome, if not memorable, sight for the long-distance walker and offers a good number of shops and a choice of accommodation.

Kington to Knighton
20 miles

Leaving Kington the Path climbs from the river past one of the highest golf courses in England to skirt Bradnor Hill. Where the route dog-legs on Rushock Hill there is a short stretch of Offa's Dyke, precursor of more to come. It now descends once more into the Vale of Radnor, then climbs again past Burfa Hill. Here the Dyke is prominent once more and there is some hard going as you descend to the Presteigne road. Ascending yet again, the Path roughly follows the line of the Dyke across rolling hill tops that offer impressive views.

And so, eventually, via some short stretches on roads, you come down into Knighton, popularly known as 'The Town on the Dyke' and tailor-made as a midway point for rest and recuperation. It was here that the Path was officially opened by Sir John Hunt in 1971, and, appropriately enough, the town also houses the headquarters of the Offa's Dyke Association. Just up the hill from the distinctive Clock Square there is an information centre and the Old Primary School in West Street has been converted to a youth hostel. Walkers with limited time frequently choose this strategic old castle town as their starting-point for tackling half the path, northwards or southwards. Knighton is not only the best source of information on the Path, it is also served by British Rail and, as the largest of the inland townships actually on the Path, has a wide choice of accommodation and plenty of shops.

Knighton to Montgomery
14 miles

The route from here starts alongside the pretty river Teme and the Offa's Dyke Park, passing an inscribed boulder of impressive size commemorating the official opening of the Path. A sharpish ascent from the sheltered green valley brings the walker to the high country and some more hard walking. From here to a point just east of Welshpool at the foot of Long Mountain is the longest almost unbroken stretch of the Dyke on the whole footpath.

Steady application is necessary now over the repeated ups and downs of the Clun Hills of Shropshire. One of the finest views of the Dyke is the reward for climbing Llanfair Hill; here, at an elevation of 1400 feet, the earthworks are at their highest point, the Path itself leading well defined across the green, partly-wooded hills. Clun, though a couple of miles east of the Path, is a favourite resting place. Picturesque

The walls of Knighton castle, destroyed at the beginning of the fifteenth century. Earlier, the Welsh had taken the town as late as 1052, and Domesday Book mentions it as unpopulated.

Opposite Knighton, known by reason of its Welsh name, Tref-y-Clawdd, as 'the town on the Dyke', seen from the south. At times, the town, which houses the headquarters of the Offa's Dyke Association, seems filled with walkers tackling the northward or southward sections of the Path.

and seemingly untouched by time, it boasts a youth hostel, pub and shops.

There is strenuous walking now from Clun to Hergan Col and then a series of flat-top ridges. Eventually, though, you descend from Clun Forest to lowland once more and the welcome sight of Montgomery after yet another wild and lonely stretch of path across a real backwater landscape. Like Clun, Montgomery seems unaffected by time's changes; sleepy and mellow, it has a charming Georgian town square. A good rest spot, the town offers shops and accommodation.

Montgomery to Llanymynech 14 miles

The route now leads into the great plain of the river Severn, with road-walking and low-lying footpaths that can make for heavy going in wet weather. The Path rises again to Long Mountain and negotiates some wooded stretches alternating with open country around Beacon Hill before dropping down again to the valley to cross the Severn at Buttington. Those who wish to visit Powis Castle can follow the detour path to Welshpool, while on the main Path it is river bank walking for much of the way to Llanymynech.

Llanymynech to Trevor 15 miles

Limestone quarries hereabouts make the way none too pretty at first, and there is some road-walking to Trefonen, where there is a pub. You soon reach the wooded Morda valley, however, and then an open ridge above Oswestry. Some quite hard walking follows in places around Selattyn Hill. Then you cross a number of tracks and roads and come within sight of Chirk Castle across the Ceiriog valley.

Some of the most massive and memorable sections of the Dyke earthworks and the last of any significance on the Path are on the hill

Right Montgomery, a border settlement for centuries until the uniting of England and Wales, today a pleasant, slumbering town.

Above The Path at Edenhope Hill, Shropshire, one of the main stretches along which the ancient Dyke and the modern route coincide. It is said that the Hill offers the best view on the entire Path.

Opposite The turbulent river Dee from the Pontcysyllte Aqueduct near Llangollen.

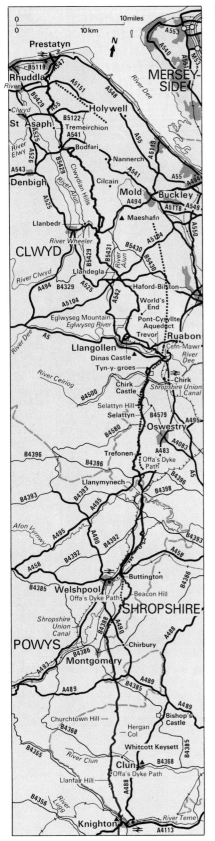

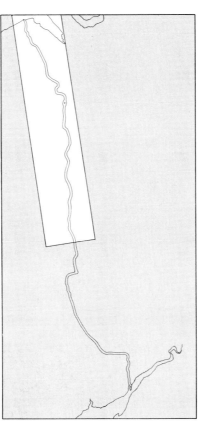

top above Nanteris. A steep drop now brings you to the Ceiriog river, which is crossed at the site of the old castle mill. An alternative path skirts the grounds and can be used when the castle is closed. The castle was completed in 1310 and has been inhabited continuously for four hundred years by the Myddleton family, who no doubt feel entitled to privacy for at least part of each year.

A scenic, uphill woodland route brings the walker to Tyn-y-groes, from where it is largely road-walking and field paths down to the Vale of Llangollen and the Dee valley. There is a tangible air of industry here, and the path turns abruptly away from the A483 to follow the Llangollen Canal towpath to the road bridge over the river Dee. An alternative route actually crosses the magnificent Pontcysyllte Aqueduct, designed and built by Thomas Telford and William Jessop between 1795 and 1805 and still carrying narrow boats and pleasure craft 120 feet above the river.

Trevor to Llandegla
11 miles

Leaving the industrial spread of Cefn-mawr and the hamlet of Trevor behind, the Path winds away north-west from the Dee and enters what is arguably the most interesting, certainly the most Welsh, section of the whole route. The Path climbs through woods, then follows a metal road variously known as the Panorama Walk and the Precipice Walk. It is impressively wild country here, notably near the Eglwyseg limestone crags.

A side path leads the walker down past the ruins of Dinas Castle into Llangollen. There are all facilities here, of course, including a youth hostel and an Information Centre. Accommodation is somewhat limited in high summer because of the number of tourists and almost impossible in July during the Eisteddfod. There are several camping-grounds on the outskirts, though. Apart from the celebrated town itself, the ruined Cistercian abbey of Valle Crucis is worth seeing.

After a short main-road section, you can follow the Eglwyseg river and rejoin the Dyke Path below the mighty Horseshoe Pass. From there the Path works its way along minor roads to the aptly-named World's End, the head of

Left Pontcysyllte Aqueduct, which carries the Llangollen Canal over the river Dee. The nineteen-arch aqueduct is just over 1000 feet long, a fine example of the skill of the early engineers of the Industrial Revolution.

Below The Eglwyseg Rocks near Llangollen towering above the Path.

the beautiful wooded valley of the river Eglwyseg. There are old lead-mine workings in the vicinity. Some hard going is needed here to reach the upland and then some very stern moorland makes constant reference to map and compass necessary.

A minor road is joined briefly at Hafod-Bilston, and then two more roads are crossed before Llandegla is reached. Most walkers are thankful to take a rest in this friendly one-street hamlet, which does, however, boast a pub, a post office and store and a camping-ground.

Llandegla to Bodfari
17 miles

Yet more stamina has to be drawn upon for the Clwydian Hills that follow Llandegla: in places the succession of rounded tops seems endless. After crossing the river Alun the Path rises, then winds across great swathes of open high country, broken by forestry plantations and several Iron Age hill-forts.

Where the Path eventually joins the A494 you may well feel like detouring west to Llanbedr, where there is a seventeenth-century inn, or east to the

Opposite The river Dee at Llangollen, home of the International Musical Eisteddfod, the annual competition for folk dancers and singers.

Opposite below Horseshoe Pass, beyond Llangollen and Valle Crucis, the Cistercian abbey founded in 1201 and dissolved by Henry VIII.

Left The country near St Asaph, a minute city with a fifteenth-century cathedral heavily restored four centuries later. The hills here are easier, and northward walkers may feel understandable relief as they near the end of their journey.

Below View of Prestatyn at the northern point of the Path.

youth hostel at Maeshafn. The Path itself continues across another succession of summits with views as far as Snowdonia on a clear day before finally descending to the river Wheeler and the quaintly-named village of Bodfari, some three miles west of Denbigh.

Bodfari to Prestatyn
10 miles

At last the going is gentler, and the walker who has tramped the length of the Path will already feel a justified sense of achievement. A mixture of pasture paths, minor roads, woodland and (in comparison with the lofty heights of the southern Clwydians) lowish foothills and scarps takes you past the diminutive cathedral city of St Asaph and the ruins of Dyserth Castle. There is a crest of fine limestone cliffs here, and the Path finishes appropriately with a splendid birds-eye view across Prestatyn and the North Wales coast. There are facilities at this popular but ugly resort, including a railway station and several miles of good beaches, but it is all a far cry from the open uplands and tough walking along the central sections of the Path.

The South-West Peninsula Coast Path

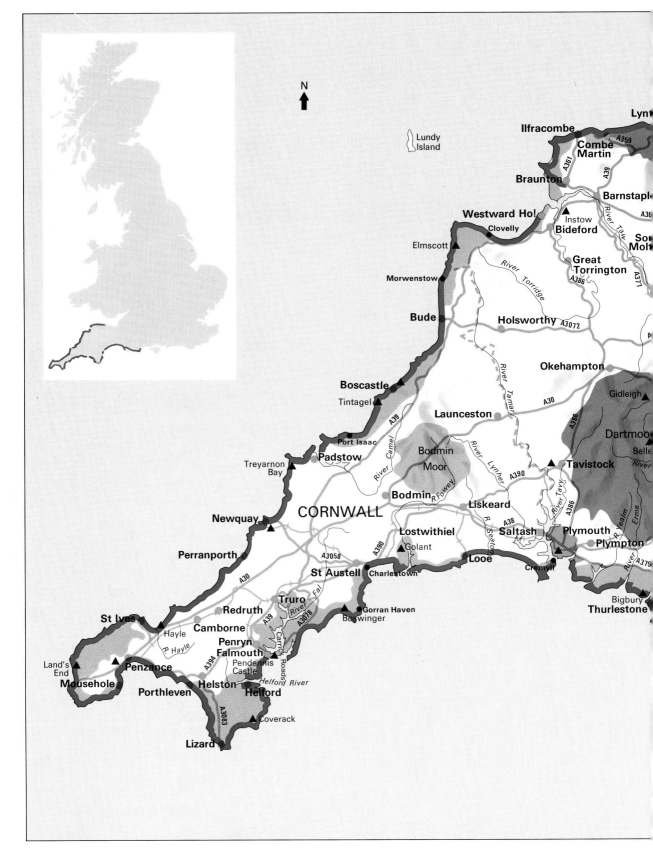

Lundy
Island

N

Lyn

Ilfracombe

Combe
Martin

A361

A39

A359

Braunton

Barnstaple

A36

Westward Ho!

Clovelly

Instow
Bideford

River Taw

So
Mol

Elmscott

Great
Torrington

A386

A371

Morwenstow

River Torridge

Bude

Holsworthy A3072

A

Okehampton

Gidleigh

Boscastle

Tintagel

River Tamar

A30

A386

Dartmoo

Belle

Launceston

Port Isaac

A39

River Camel

Bodmin
Moor

River Lynher

Tavistock

River

Padstow

River Lynher

Treyarnon
Bay

A390

A386

River Tavy

Bodmin R.Fowey

Liskeard

Plymouth

CORNWALL

R. Seaton

A38

Saltash

Plympton

Newquay

Lostwithiel

R Fowey

Golant

Looe

River Yealm

Perranporth

A3058

Cremyll

River Erme

A30

St Austell

Charlestown

Bigbury

St Ives

Redruth

Truro

River Fal

Gorran Haven

Boswinger

Thurlestone

River Plym

A379

Camborne

A39

A3078

Hayle

Penryn
Falmouth

Carrick Roads

Land's
End

R. Hayle

A394

Pendennis
Castle

Mousehole

Penzance

Helford River

Porthleven

Helston

Helford

A3083

Coverack

Lizard

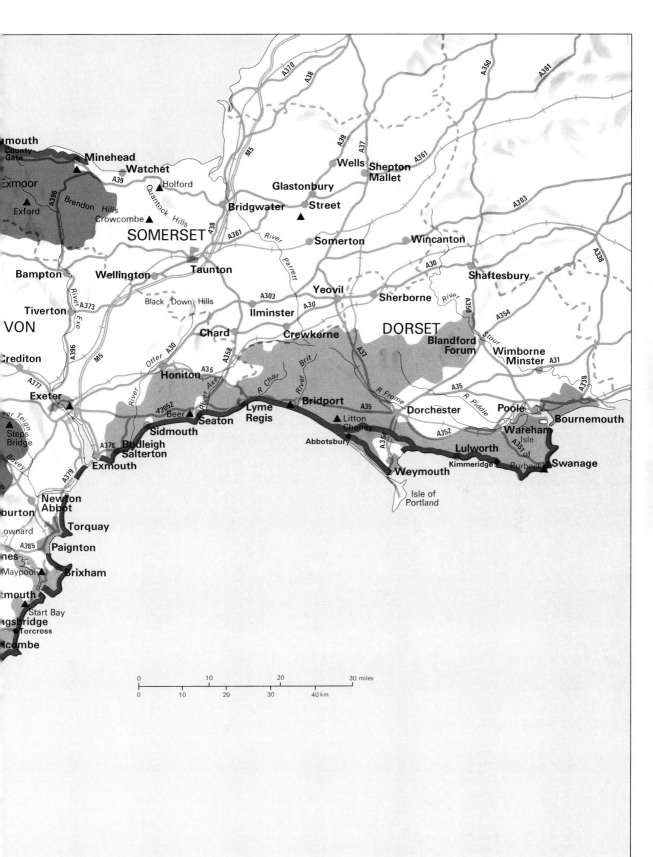

Officially approved progressively between the 1950s and 1974

Length: 515 miles excluding interruptions

Going: medium/easy

Ordnance Survey maps: 180, 181, 190, 192, 193, 194, 195, 200, 201, 202, 203 and 204

From Minehead in Somerset to the edge of Poole harbour in Dorset, the South-West Peninsula Coast Path takes the walker along an impressive, and often wild and lonely, coastline. Much of the fascination of the Path lies in the distinctive character, landscape and climate of the four counties through which it passes. Though comparatively short, the Somerset stretch has some magnificent moments, among them Porlock Hill and the Exmoor uplands. North Devon offers charming harbours at Lynmouth and Clovelly and the wide, white sands of Woolacombe Bay, South Devon the softer delights of the Dart valley and the film-set beauty of Salcombe. In Cornwall the contrasts could hardly be greater: Atlantic breakers hurling themselves on to the rocky northern shore and a series of snuggling havens on the Channel coast. Dorset is different yet again, wide and surprisingly remote, with some outstandingly dramatic sections around St Alban's Head and to both east and west of Lulworth cove.

Even the most dedicated walkers are unlikely to tackle the whole Path in one expedition: at 515 miles it is the longest long-distance path in Great Britain and more than twice as long as the Pennine Way, its nearest rival. Yet whichever section is chosen, the walker will discover fine views and a true sense of exhilaration.

The Path is a genuine coastal route. It hugs the cliffs whenever possible, veering inland only occasionally and then usually remaining within sound, if not sight, of the sea. There are a number of interruptions, however, most notably around Torbay (where most walkers will prefer to take public transport through the substantial built-up area) and at Lulworth, where an alternative path must be followed when the firing ranges are in use. Numerous estuaries also create a number of other, more pleasant, diversions, especially around Barnstaple, Falmouth and Plymouth.

Somerset and North Devon

Minehead to County Gate
8 miles

Minehead makes a pleasant starting-point for the walker. The town has an unhurried air, except perhaps in the height of the season, there is ample accommodation, and parking should not be difficult to arrange.

The Path itself begins rather casually, winding upwards from the end of Minehead quay, with little as yet to suggest the magnificent scenery ahead. The wooded ascent is pleasant enough, however, once the municipal tipping-ground on the seaward side has been passed. The Path soon steepens and then levels out to cross North Hill. Superb high-level walking follows towards Selworthy Beacon, where the viewpoint, 1013 feet above sea level, is worth a slight detour.

There is now a short length of road walking through the pretty hamlet of Bossington. Then, having reached sea level, the Path follows the beach to Porlock Weir, a charming cluster of cottages around a steep walled harbour with a mellow inn and a few shops.

The Path now bears due west and gradually begins to climb again alongside Yearnor Wood, then continues on the cliff tops high above the sea. Culbone has the tiniest church in England, reached only by footpath and delightfully secluded in a wooded glade. It can hold a congregation of no more than sixteen. Lanes and wood-land paths take the walker through Broomstreet and Yenworthy and so to the Somerset/Devon border on the A39

at County Gate. There is a large car park here and an information centre.

County Gate to Lynmouth
7 miles

After topping Cosgate Hill and crossing an area of open land, the walker has to follow the A39 for a short way. Care is needed here, for the road carries heavy traffic in the summer. The route soon veers seaward to skirt Kipscombe Hill and cross Countisbury Common. This is another fine stretch of country, and a couple of paths lead out to Foreland Point lighthouse. The Path joins the A39 again for the steep descent into Lynmouth.

Lynmouth is a logical place for a rest, for it is not only a charming and attractive little town, but facilities for the traveller are first class. There is a youth hostel at Lynton, Lynmouth's twin town on top of the cliffs, and a well-run little camping-ground at nearby Lynbridge. Comprehensive local information is available from the National Park Centre in Lynmouth.

Lynmouth to Combe Martin
12 miles

A stiff climb heralds the start of the route again, over Hollerday Hill and then on through the spectacular Valley of Rocks, a huge natural arena set amid fern-clad hills to the south and some grotesque peaks of rock on the seaward side. The Path now hugs a narrow toll road for a couple of miles, skirting a section of cliff that is sheer in places. Then it leaves the fine open scenery behind and plunges into the trees towards the aptly-named Woody Bay, where the beach is good for swimming.

From here a track takes the walker through thickly wooded slopes, gaps in the trees providing glimpses of the shore. It may perhaps be better to keep to the metalled road, for the cliff path is considered unsafe. Past the turn-off to Martinhoe Mansion the Path joins an old coach road, now a green track, which provides easy walking over a well-graded surface.

There are magnificent landscapes as the Path winds around Martinhoe Beacon, eventually dropping into a steep and beautiful combe to reach the Hunter's Inn near the mouth of the river Heddon. It is otter and badger country here, wild and secretive away from the roads and tracks.

The Path returns to the cliffs to round Trentishoe Down and Hold-stone Down. Then a wide track leads the walker over Knap Down, past Great and Little Hangman and down into Combe Martin, a straggling town nestling in a combe dominated on each side by towering cliffs. The Path emerges at a municipal car-park, where the Exmoor Information Centre is open during the summer.

Combe Martin to Ilfracombe
6 miles

Between Combe Martin and Ilfracombe some rights of way along the cliffs remain to be negotiated, although a route for the footpath is gradually being established. At the moment the walker has to follow the A399 and part of an old coaching road past Water-mouth Castle, a neo-Gothic mansion complete with a minstrels' gallery and a smugglers' tunnel. From here it is a pleasant walk past the tiny cove of

Hele, around Beacon Point and then down into Ilfracombe.

Ilfracombe to Braunton
15 miles

One of the delights of most West Country resorts is the absence of suburbs, and Ilfracombe, though large by Devon standards, is no exception. The Path starts again just west of the town centre and climbs above the impressive harbour to turn west along Torrs Walk. This is easy walking with views across the Bristol Channel. The Path narrows after passing Shag Point, rugged cliffs to seaward and golf links inland. Navigating around Bull Point can be slightly confusing; keep to the higher path just inland if in doubt.

You can either round Morte Point on the official Path or take the southerly track from Rockham Bay into Mort-hoe, an historic village said to have been the home of one of Thomas à Becket's murderers. The Point itself is

now owned by the National Trust. In the days of sail it was a seafarer's nightmare: during one winter no less than five ships were wrecked on its treacherous rocks.

It is largely road walking into Woola-combe, which has a pleasant prome-nade and a splendid silver-sand beach, one of the best in the West Country and crowded with holidaymakers through-out the summer months. From here the Path remains mainly on roads, but you can walk along the beach towards Baggy Point and the high sand dunes of Saunton instead. A short distance inland is Braunton, which marks the first major interruption in the Path.

Braunton to Westward Ho!
19 miles

From Braunton the walker must make his way inland around the wide estuary of the rivers Taw and Torridge through Barnstaple and Bideford.

Barnstaple is a pleasant old town,

Opposite Watermouth Castle, unlike many of the places passed by the South-West Peninsula Coast Path not an ancient site with legendary associations but a nineteenth-century neo-Gothic creation complete with minstrels' gallery and smugglers' tunnel.

Left Ilfracombe, the largest resort along the North Devon coast, built around a pleasant old harbour.

Above Woolacombe Bay, a fine 2-mile-long surfing beach crowded in high summer with holidaymakers.

Top The Path just west of Westward Ho!, a tiny, unvisited spot until Charles Kingsley's novel made it famous.

Above Boscastle Harbour, a tiny inlet set amid hostile cliffs. There has been a settlement here since the twelfth century.

and the modern civic centre is the only discordant note amid the old buildings of the town. Its most famous landmark is the great sixteen-arch Bridge across the Taw. Bideford can be avoided if the summer ferry between Instow (where there is a youth hostel) and Appledore is running. The picturesque town is worth a visit, though, and along the quay fishermen and sea-

men still gather as they have for centuries.

Thanks to Charles Kingsley's novel of Elizabethan adventure, after which the town was named, Westward Ho! evokes romantic visions of tall ships and dramatic heroism. Sadly reality is somewhat different, a rash of chalets and commercialism. But the shore compensates for the man-made medio-

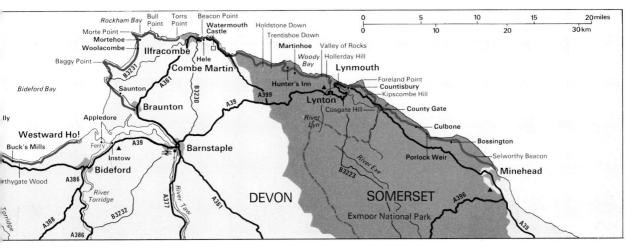

crity, great Atlantic breakers crashing in over the superb sands, a surfer's paradise.

Westward Ho! to Marsland Mouth
15 miles

From the western end of the housing development the Path follows an old coast road over National Trust land. The views across the great sweep of Bideford Bay are quite marvellous: Clovelly nestling in the centre, Hartland Point in the distance and the unmistakeable shape of Lundy Island even further off to the north-west. There is cliff walking to Worthygate Wood and then much steep going up and down the combes, through Buck's Mills and on to Clovelly, its cobbled streets hanging from the edge of the cliff. Tourism has all but spoilt the village; try to arrive here very early in the day or—better still—out of season.

From Clovelly to Hartland Point and beyond there is a fair amount of hard going. The Path is not always easy to follow and in places heavy undergrowth obstructs the way. There have also been a number of cliff falls. You may want to turn inland to Hartland village where there is accommodation and a friendly little camping-ground. The Path may then be rejoined at Hartland Quay. There is a youth hostel at Elmscott.

The stretch from Hartland Quay to the Devon/Cornwall border at Marsland Mouth is one of the most majestic and rugged along the whole route, with seabirds wheeling above the foaming waves. The walker will notice that gradually the scenery is beginning to alter. The cliffs are more jagged, the woods are less frequent, the villages

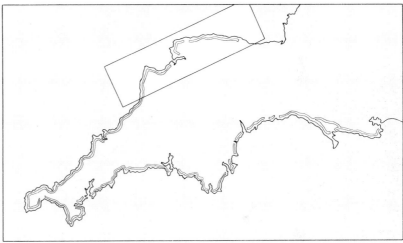

smaller and rarer, the combes not quite so luxuriant: already Cornwall is making its geological mark.

The steep, cobbled streets of Clovelly, now all but ruined by twee tourist shops and cafes.

Cornwall
Marsland Mouth to Bude
19 miles

The first miles in Cornwall can be a memorable experience, especially if the clouds are scudding and white caps are freckling the sea. Stunted trees battered by the relentless westerlies cling desperately to the granite cliff tops. It is not the easiest of walking, for much scrambling in and out of ravines is necessary, and the Path is ill-defined in places and often obscured with bracken. The vigorous will respond to the challenge, however, particularly if they have paused to bathe from the secluded beach at Welcombe, on the Devon side of the boundary.

Most people make a short detour inland to Morwenstow. Here there is a

Above The castle at Tintagel, built in the twelfth century but long since dedicated in the popular imagination to King Arthur.

Above right Bude, a fine surfing resort strategically placed as a starting-point for walkers tackling the north Cornwall stretch of the Peninsula Path.

picturesque pub close to the charming little church where Robert Stephen Hawker, the famous poet and eccentric, was vicar for over forty years. Many of the graves in the graveyard are of drowned sailors, a reminder of the harsh coast nearby.

After some road walking, the last couple of miles into Bude provide smooth and easy going over sheep-cropped grass and some superb panoramas. Despite being one of the country's greatest surfing centres and a very popular resort, Bude has retained much of its mellow dignity. The tide rises very high here, so bathing other than in the recommended areas is inadvisable.

Bude to Boscastle Harbour
15 miles

The route is a mixture of path and road now, and the going is easy at first as far as Widemouth Sands, where surfers disport themselves among some of the biggest combers in Britain. On the ascent to Dizzard Point the terrain becomes rougher, however. There is a fine descent to the tiny cove of Crackington Haven, followed immediately by a mile-long haul to Cambeak Point. It is hard going around

Pentargon Cove, but the Path becomes easier as it descends to Boscastle Harbour, which is old Cornwall as one has always imagined it, rugged cliffs enclosing a peaceful haven.

Boscastle Harbour to Port Isaac
12 miles

The route from Boscastle Harbour to Tintagel is one of the best cliff walks in the whole peninsula. It is marvellous going over springy turf, the Path flirting with the cliff edge, dipping into ravines and offering splendid views seawards, even occasionally downwards. At Tintagel the ruins of the twelfth-century castle–popularly but unjustifiably linked with King Arthur–attract crowds of tourists. Almost as fascinating is the fourteenth-century Old Post Office, originally built as a medieval manor.

Between Tintagel and Port Isaac sections of the Path are quite rough, notably around Dennis Point, and you may want to take to inland lanes and rejoin the Path above Tregardock Beach. The route is more clearly defined as it descends to the lower cliffs at Port Gaverne, from where it is largely road-walking into Port Isaac, a lovely unspoiled **fishing village**. There are some modern bungalows on the upper slopes, but the harbour remains intact, a tiny beach, narrow streets, walls washed in bright colours and the constant tang of salt spray all sustaining a real seafaring atmosphere.

Port Isaac to Padstow
12 miles

There is no access to the cliff path out of Port Isaac, and the walker has to cut inland to Port Quin and Doyden Point. From there the Path marches on towards Pentire Point and past a host of thrusting headlands and swooping clefts before descending to the shore

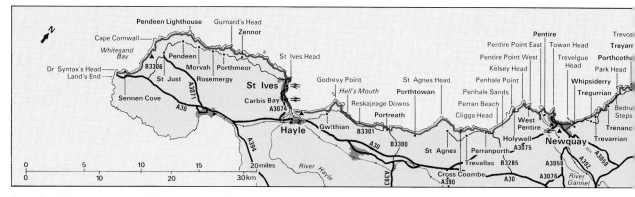

Right Sand-dune country near Hayle. Progress may be slow here, for the terrain impedes brisk walking.

Below Bedruthan Steps, one of which, known as Queen Bess Rock, is said to resemble Queen Elizabeth I's profile.

Below right The appropriately named Hell's Mouth, one of the most awesome moments along this spectacular coast.

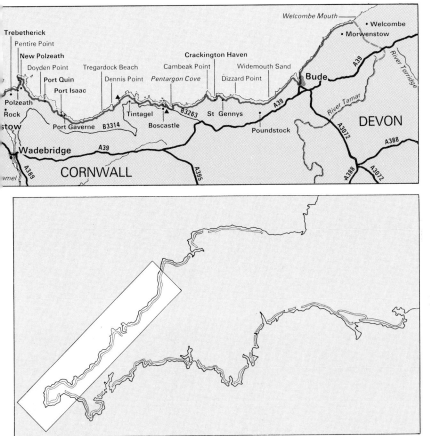

Newquay to Perranporth
12 miles

The walker crosses the river Gannel either by ferry or by footbridge and follows the Path towards Perranporth over a stretch largely consisting of sand dunes. In the middle of Penhale Sands is St Piran's church. One of the oldest in the country, it is at least 1,300 years old and was saved from total burial by drifting sand during the last century. From St Piran's church the Path now runs along Perran Beach to Perranporth, a holiday resort with excellent surfing.

Perranporth to St Ives
28 miles

There are fine views as you round St Agnes Head, from where it is easy going to the steep cove of Portreath. A short stretch on roads now precedes another invigorating walk across the Icelandic-sounding Reskajeage Downs and over grand cliffs, most notably the satanic Hell's Mouth.

Below Godrevy Point there are more sand dunes. The Path turns inland briefly to pass through Gwithian and then runs three miles or more above a splendid beach. You may want to stop to enjoy the sands, for Hayle, a distinctly unpretty working town, is no fun to walk through, and nor are the following few miles around Carbis Bay to St Ives.

This only serves to emphasize the charm of St Ives itself, one of the most colourful ports in the country and understandably a focal point for artists. The labyrinthine steep streets, cobbled passageways and old cottages are a riot of colour. When the sun shines there is more than a touch of Italy here.

St Ives to Land's End
22 miles

If you have had a surfeit of holiday crowds you will relish the next stretch to Cape Cornwall, some 16 miles of rugged and virtually unpeopled coastline, a landscape of rough moor, jutting rocks and bracken. The Path is hard going in places, often vague and heavily overgrown in others, an irresistible challenge to experienced walkers.

If you want to divert inland, do so at Zennor, where there is a pub. The church has a fine square tower and within a wealth of finely proportioned stone arches and a fourteenth-century font. Carved into the end of one of the

and the holiday strip around Polzeath. From here it is well defined walking through sand dunes along the estuary of the river Camel to Rock, where there is a regular ferry service to Padstow.

Padstow to Newquay
16 miles

From Padstow the Path passes a succession of beaches along gentle cliffs. Before Newquay is reached there are some outstanding rock formations, most notably Bedruthan Steps, a series of rocky islets along the shore, said to have been stepping-stones used by the legendary giant Bedruthan. Keep well back from the edge of the cliffs, for there are some well-disguised overhangs.

Newquay, not long ago merely a few cottages grouped around a tiny fishing harbour, is now the largest resort in Cornwall and appropriately sophisticated. The magnificent coastline remains unspoilt, however. Huer's House on the distinctive headland was used by look-outs watching for mackerel shoals.

St Ives, once a port for working fishermen, now a holiday centre and artists' colony. Whistler and Sickert visited in the nineteenth century, and more recently Ben Nicholson, Barbara Hepworth and Bernard Leach have made their homes here.

benches is the Mermaid of Zennor, said to have lured many a sailor on to the rocks. There is a memorial stone on the wall to one John Davey, the last man to speak true Cornish.

From Zennor there is a fine path, one followed for hundreds of years by Cornishmen who think it prudent to walk half a mile inland from the savage sea and treacherous cliffs. Near Morvah, the Path deteriorates again, and it is best to take the road from Rosemergy through Morvah and rejoin the Path near Pendeen lighthouse. Cape Cornwall, where there is a coast-guard station and a hotel, is a wild and

lonely place, desolate in winter but attractive under the summer sun.

Around St Just the effects of the tin-mining industry on the landscape are all too obvious. The Path curves around Whitesand Bay, providing fine views of the curiously-named Dr Syntax's Head and the Longships lighthouse, and then drops down to Sennen Cove. Although hardly a jewel among Cornish harbours, this is an honest and purposeful fishing haven that has largely resisted commercialization.

Only a couple of miles separate Sennen and Land's End, but they are enough to absorb the dramatic atmo-

sphere of Britain's westernmost point. You can almost visualize the tiny ships of old sailing past to half a world away. It is said that those who can sail around Britain, with her high tides and dangerous coasts, can sail anywhere. Nowhere is this more apparent than at Land's End where the Atlantic hurls itself ceaselessly at the massive granite cliffs.

So much for the romance of Land's End. The reality is a clutter of development and endless crowds in summer. Just a few steps along the coast path, however, the walker is once again amid natural and majestic beauty.

Land's End to Mousehole
15 miles

The first section of the route through south Cornwall, from Land's End to Mousehole (pronounced 'Mouzel'), is a succession of delights. There are two paths along the whole stretch; one follows every contour of the cliff, while the other cuts across most of the headlands.

Between Gwennap Head and Porthgwarra Cove you may, if you are lucky, see seals, for this part of the coast is one of their favourite haunts. After St Levan you reach the Minack Cliff open-air theatre, where plays are

Land's End, the English mainland's most westerly spot and a significant turning-point for walkers on the South-West Peninsula Coast Path. To the north lies the turbulent, wind-swept Atlantic shore, southwards the gentler peace of the Channel coast.

Performance at the Minack Cliff Theatre near Porthcurno, perched high in the cliff face. The annual summer season of plays is world famous.

staged during the summer among the rocks. Then comes Porthcurno beach, scattered with thousands of shells, followed by a really beautiful stretch of country towards Logan Rock. This massive 65-ton boulder, which lies just off the main Path, is so delicately balanced on top of a rugged outcrop that it can be rocked by hand.

Further on, Lamorna valley is particularly attractive, and the cove, as charming as its name, has become something of an artists' colony: there is a grand old pub called 'The Wink'. After a few more miles the Path reaches Mousehole, once described as the perfect Cornish fishing village and still a huddle of cosy cottages cascading down to the harbour.

Mousehole to Porthleven
18 miles

The Path breaks here, leaving the walker to find his own way through Penzance. It begins again at the less attractive eastern end of town, but only as road for the first few miles through Marazion and past St Michael's Mount, which can be reached at low tide across a causeway.

The Path now climbs towards Prussia Cove, twisting tortuously in places, and then leads on to Praa Sands, a mile-long golden strand and a holiday-maker's delight. From here there is another stiffish climb to Trewavas Head, and so the walker comes to Porthleven, a small fishing village with an impressively long jetty.

Opposite Mousehole harbour, still with much of the atmosphere of a traditional Cornish fishing village. Mousehole, like Zennor on the north coast, lays claim to the last person of Cornish mother tongue, one Dolly Pentreath, who died in 1777.

Top St Michael's Mount. The twelfth-century castle was built on the site of a Benedictine priory, a daughter house of the monastery on Mont Saint-Michel, off the Breton coast.

Above Mevagissey, most charming of all the harbours along the south Cornish coast, another popular spot with anglers and artists.

Porthleven to Lizard
11 miles

Just beyond Porthleven is Loe Bar, a shinglebank enclosing a natural fresh water lake, the biggest in the peninsula. The Path runs along soft, serpentine cliffs to Poldhu Cove and on to the cliff-top monument that marks the spot where in 1901 Marconi made the first trans-Atlantic wireless transmission.

There has been considerable development in and around Mullion Cove recently, but nevertheless the tiny harbour with its cave and the Gull Rock remains serene. A few **miles** further on at Kynance, there **may well**

be large crowds in summer, come to admire the strange formations of serpentine rock and the natural grandeur of the cove. Fortunately much of the surrounding land is now in the protective ownership of the National Trust.

From Kynance the Path runs well marked across a magnificent stretch of coast dotted with forbidding rocky headlands. The view inland across the desolate Lizard Peninsula is by contrast rather dull. Most walkers make a brief diversion to Lizard town, now largely dependent on the tourist trade.

Lizard to Falmouth
26 miles

The walking on the eastern side of the peninsula is easier, although the coves are neither so numerous nor so spectacular. Cadgwith is a pretty fishing village, however, and Carleon Cove a recognized beauty spot.

After Kennack Sands there are

rugged cliffs all the way past Black Head to Coverack, where the Path turns inland to avoid quarry workings. It returns to the coast briefly before going inland once again along lanes and tracks to Porthallow Cove. Beyond Nare Point the tiny estuary at Gillan Harbour can be crossed at low tide; at high tide it is necessary to follow the river a little way inland and cross the bridge at Carne.

The Path then rounds Dennis Head and follows Helford river inland to Helford, where the ferry must be taken across the estuary. From here some 8 miles of easy, pleasant walking around Rosemullion Head and Pennance Point are necessary to reach Falmouth.

Falmouth to Gorran Haven
17 miles

From this bustling and picturesque seaport, where Pendennis Castle, built by Henry VIII, stands sentinel over the entrance to Carrick Roads, two ferries in quick succession must be taken to reach St Anthony in Roseland and the continuation of the Path. The first connects Falmouth and St Mawes, the second, which runs less regularly, plies across the estuary of Percuil river to St Anthony.

Above Kynance Cove, where the caves, blow-holes and multi-coloured serpentine rock attract crowds of visitors.

Top right An outcrop of the 'Cornish Alps' near St Austell. Some of the spoil heaps rise 300 feet or more, evidence of what remains, along with tourism, one of Cornwall's most important industries.

Right The harbour at Polperro. The inlet is so narrow that in bad weather baulks of timber can be placed across the entrance.

There is good walking around Zone Point and Gerrans Bay across lowish cliffs to pretty Portloe, followed by a rather stiffer stretch around the western side of Veryan Bay. Gently wooded slopes follow, a contrast with the open country left behind at Porthluney Cove.

Behind the cove stands Caerhays Castle, built in the early nineteenth century by John Nash, the celebrated Regency architect who also rebuilt Buckingham Palace and Brighton Pavilion. Now comes the assault on the massive Dodman Point, a headland of treacherous rocks topped by an ancient granite cross, followed by a steep descent to the snug harbour at Gorran Haven.

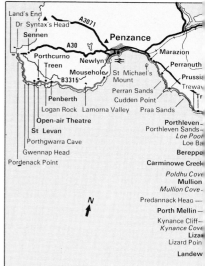

Above Looe harbour and the Victorian bridge joining the eastern and western parts of the town.

Right Salcombe, where orange, lemon and palm trees grow in an atmosphere that belongs more to southern Europe than to southern England.

Gorran Haven to Par Sands
16 miles

The hills become more friendly and softer now, and between Porthmellon and Mevagissey the Path is tarmac. There are splendid views over the town, one of the main tourist centres in Cornwall.

From Mevagissey a well-defined track leads around a lovely stretch of coast past Penare Point and down to Pentewan Sands, where there is a camping-site on the beach. The sea here is often made a brilliant azure by the outspill from the china-clay mines near St Austell. Around Black Head the Path is especially remote and beautiful, but as it approaches St Austell signs of industry and tourism increase. The peaks of spoil—nicknamed the 'Cornish Alps'—will form the backdrop to the walk for quite some time now. The Path skirts St Austell itself, running seaward through Charlestown and Par Sands.

Par Sands to Looe
18 miles

From Par Sands the Path runs along some impressive cliffs between Polkerris and Fowey. As the walker rounds Gribbin Head and approaches

the estuary he will enjoy some fine views over Fowey, a fascinating old town with steep and cobbled streets and a small port. No less enchanting is Polruan, a short ferry journey away on the other side of the estuary. Here the streets are even narrower, though in Fowey you would hardly have believed that possible.

There are 6 tough miles of lovely cliff walk now, with few escape routes once you have started. It is a magnificent coast, though, and well worth the effort. The Path passes Pencarrow Head and Lantivet Bay and then descends across National Trust land to Polperro, where the celebrated harbour claims more than its fair share of visitors.

Between Polperro and Looe, there are numerous holiday developments, but the Path winds serenely on around

Talland Bay and then joins the coast road to run down to the harbour. The two parts of the town, East and West Looe, are linked by a fine bridge. Thronged with holidaymakers throughout the summer, Looe is renowned as a shark-fishing centre.

Looe to Cremyll
21 miles

The Path now hugs the cliffs to Portwrinkle, dog-legs around an army range and returns to the coast to run along Whitesand Bay to Rame Head. Holiday chalets mar the landscape here, but the last stretch of the Cornish section of the Path more than makes up for that, for the view across the estuary of the Tamar is regal. Skirting Edgcumbe Park, the walker finally reaches the ferry across the sound to Plymouth at Cremyll.

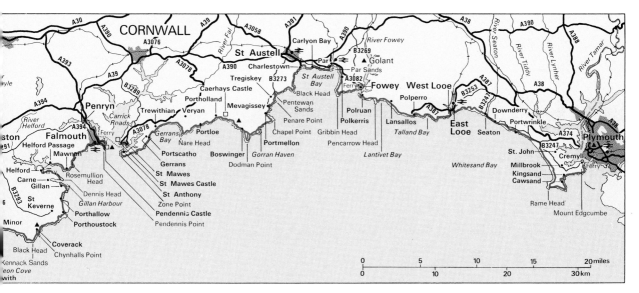

South Devon

Plymouth to Thurlestone
17 miles

Plymouth must surely be one of the most impressive cities in the country, the very hub of Britain's maritime history. Here Drake awaited the Spanish Armada in 1588, and from here in 1620 the *Mayflower* sailed, taking the Pilgrim Fathers to the New World. For many years the city was the greatest of all the nation's naval bases.

Today much has changed. A gleaming new civic centre has replaced the old heart of the town, destroyed by wartime bombing. Something of old Plymouth remains in the Barbican, however, where the narrow Elizabethan streets and fishing quays remind the visitor of the city's illustrious past. The excellent Maritime Museum is also well worth a visit.

The Path resumes on the eastern side of the city. The contrast with the wild and windswept coastline of Cornwall is immediately obvious, for the water laps gently here and the atmosphere is balmy. Winding its way around the low cliffs of Jennycliff Bay, the Path reaches Bovisand Bay, a popular holiday spot and sub-aqua centre.

At Heybrook Bay, locals will point out the modest guest-house facing the beach where Terence Rattigan wrote *French Without Tears*. There is good walking from here to the river Yealm, which is crossed by a ferry that runs at reasonable hours.

The Path now runs through woodland at first and then across the steep,

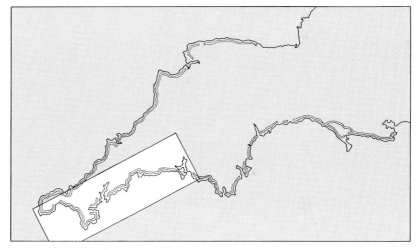

bracken-carpeted slopes of Beacon Hill, broken up with sheer cliffs and cragy fissures. At Mothecombe, where there are still problems about the right of way, most walkers head inland and return to the Path a few miles further on at Thurlestone. This means missing the estuaries of the Erme and Avon and also Bigbury-on-Sea, but unless you are fond of brash resorts this will be no great hardship.

Thurlestone to Salcombe
8 miles

Thurlestone heralds one of the most spectacular and regal stretches of the whole Devon route, across National Trust land from Bolt Tail over Bolberry Down and The Warren to Bolt Head. The descent from the lofty tops through the heavily wooded slopes and down into Salcombe is pure delight.

This is Devon's most celebrated small-boat estuary, and the annual regatta is made the more impressive by the outstandingly beautiful setting.

Salcombe to Dartmouth
21 miles

Another ferry transports you from Salcombe to East Portlemouth. The Path now follows fine open cliffs to Prawle Point, the southernmost tip of Devon, and on to Start Point. Here, by the lighthouse and just seaward of the transmitter pylons, the long descent to Start Bay begins.

On the way into Torcross there are good views of Slapton Ley, a huge freshwater lake separated from the sea by Slapton Sands, a narrow spit of beach. The Path runs along the foreshore and then climbs steeply to Strete, running for some of the way

Right Bolt Head, where the Path turns north after following a treacherous stretch of coast that has claimed many ships and men.

Below right View over Dartmouth, one of Devon's loveliest towns. There is a wealth of history here, including a fifteenth-century castle and a number of attractive buildings dating from the seventeenth century.

along an old coaching road. It then passes Blackpool Sands, an attractive beach, and the village of Stoke Fleming.

From here there is a well-trodden section around Blackstone Point and down to the Dart, Devon's loveliest river, by Dartmouth Castle. Dartmouth was an important port as long ago as the eleventh century, and Richard the Lionheart left for the Crusades from here in 1190. Now the town is the home of the illustrious Royal Naval College.

Dartmouth to Torbay
13 miles

The Lower Ferry takes the walker across the Dart to Kingswear and provides a colourful view back to the waterfront at Dartmouth. An inland diversion follows now, and the coast is not regained until Man Sands. From here the Path winds around St Mary's Bay, passing a number of holiday camps *en route* to Berry Head. There are superb views on the descent to Brixham. Despite the rash of bungalows on the edge of town, the old town and the harbour are much as they were a century ago. An imposing statue on the quay commemorates William of Orange, who landed here in 1688.

Though there is a three-mile section of official Path from Brixham to Goodrington Sands, most walkers will admit that the best walking is over for the moment and will use public transport to get through Torbay. Not that Paignton and Torquay are unattractive; Torquay in particular is a genuinely elegant town. But for all its pockets of beauty Torbay is not for the serious walker.

Torbay to Exmouth
16 miles

The official Path starts again near Hope's Nose, but only north of Maidencombe, east of Torquay, is the built-up area left behind. There is a short spell of road walking at Labrador Bay before an impressive but brief

Slapton Sands, used in 1943 by American troops to rehearse the storming of the similar Normandy beaches the following year.

stretch of cliff path brings the walker down to Shaldon and the ferry across the river Teign. Here there is yet another interruption, some five miles long, save for a short stretch on the approach to the river Exe near Dawlish Warren station. Just beyond here it is necessary to make one's way inland to Starcross for the ferry to Exmouth.

Exmouth to Sidmouth
10 miles

The footpath resumes about a mile eastwards of the busy harbour, skirts an enormous holiday camp at Sandy Bay and then detours around an army firing range before running along the distinctive red cliffs known as The Floors. It is easy walking now over a well-defined path into Budleigh Salterton, a picturesque little resort that has not been over-commercialized. Millais painted his famous picture *The Boyhood of Raleigh* here, and the great navigator, statesman and author was born just a little way inland, at Hayes Barton.

East of the town the Path works its way around the mouth of the river Otter, then heads seawards again to

Otterton Point and on to Ladram Bay. Ladram Bay is a charming inlet, not greatly marred by a holiday site, with an outcrop of intriguing red-sand rocks just offshore. The Path passes the appropriately-named Three Rocks Inn and starts to climb Peak Hill. The ascent is wooded and gradual at first, then fiercer and more open as the heights are reached. This is one of the most spectacular hills in south Devon: magnificent red cliffs, superb views and genuinely exhilarating as the walker gains the summit and begins the downward rush into Sidmouth. Long before the walker enters Sidmouth there are fascinating views over the town. Like Budleigh and Seaton, further along the Path, Sidmouth is remarkably quiet for a seaside resort, its tourist attractions commendably restrained.

Sidmouth to Lyme Regis
19 miles

A well-used bridle path begins the next stretch, past the sailing club and along a pleasing stretch of coast to Branscombe Cove, set in a deep combe. The ruddy ochre of the cliffs gives way to white around Beer Head, and the Path, though decidedly up and down at times, is well defined. Beer, famous for lace-making and smuggling, is a tiny harbour dominated by

towering cliffs. From Beer there is a brisk cliff-top walk through a more or less urban area to Seaton.

There is another break in the official route through Seaton, but the walker simply follows the promenade and crosses the river Axe on the road bridge. The Path then climbs across the golf course before entering the famous 5-mile landslip. This is exactly what you would expect it to be: a vast area in which, on Christmas Day 1839, the cliff slid into the sea, leaving a ridge path below the original cliff top. Once you have entered the landslip there is no escape until you reach the outskirts of Lyme Regis, and you must be ready for some three or four hours of heavy going over a narrow path much overgrown in places. As you leave the landslip, you also leave Devon behind and begin another precipitous descent into Dorset and historic Lyme Regis.

Dorset

Lyme Regis to Seatown
6 miles

Lyme Regis makes a pleasant starting-place for the Dorset section of the Peninsula Path. The town is charming, with a steep and narrow main street rising from the picturesque harbour, Georgian houses and attractive cottages, all surrounded by grand cliffs.

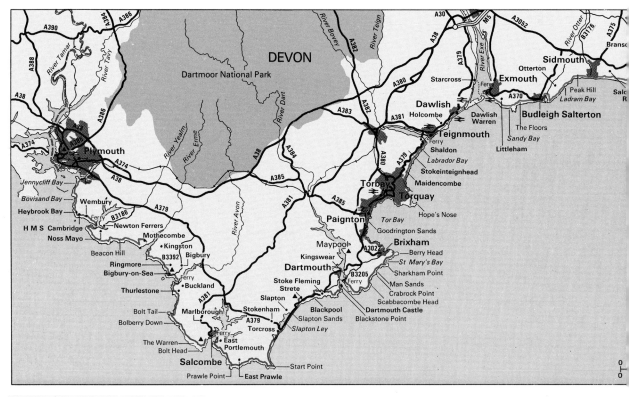

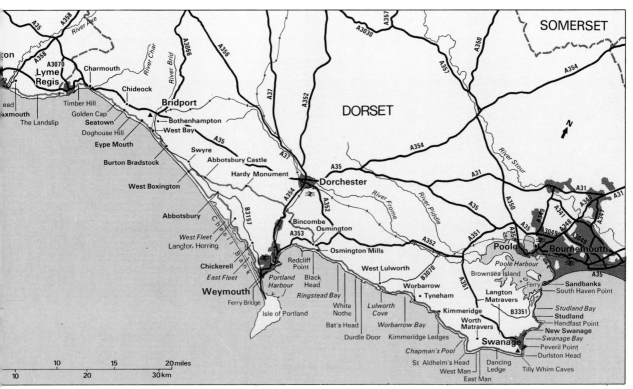

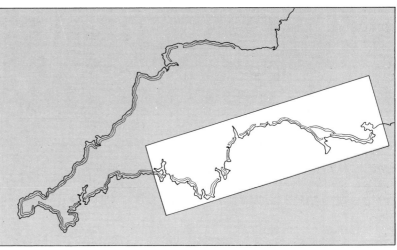

The coast near Lulworth. This section of the Path through Dorset is an exhilarating, stamina-testing switchback walk.

The fine walking over Timber Hill to Charmouth gives a foretaste of the country to come. Like Lyme, Charmouth is a popular resort, but walkers will see little of the town unless they make a slight detour. The Path crosses the river Char by a footbridge on the beach and then gradually begins to climb to Golden Cap, at 618 feet the highest point on the south coast. Its sandstone cap really does shine gold in the sunlight, and it can be seen from as far east as the Hardy Monument. Tiny Seatown, with its one pub, cluster of cottages and small caravan site, is reached after a steep descent.

Seatown to Abbotsbury
16 miles

A series of round-topped hills now brings the walker to Bridport. Past Doghouse Hill, a giant's switchback, the Path runs through Eype Mouth and down to West Bay, still a pleasant little working port, although rapidly becoming a resort. This section is one of the most magnificent in the entire 500-mile route.

There is a long walk now at sea level through Burton Bradstock towards Chesil Beach. Some three miles east of Burton Bradstock, there is a choice of routes. The main Path heads inland and up over the roof of Dorset, passes the Hardy Monument (commemorating Nelson's lieutenant, not the Wessex novelist) and then sweeps through the countryside behind Weymouth, meeting the coast again well east of Weymouth at Osmington Mills. It is a splendid landscape, but the Path is a long haul and often ill-

defined.

Walkers who want to see Chesil Beach will press on past West Bexington along the foreshore. The Path then turns inland a little to Abbotsbury. Visitors come here from all over the world to see the famous swannery, in which over 500 swans are kept. The village is a charming huddle of mellow stone houses with thatched roofs. There is a fine fifteenth-century tithe barn, and the seaman's chapel of St Catherine stands lonely and beautifully preserved on a nearby hilltop.

Abbotsbury to Weymouth
13 miles

The route is somewhat hazy east of Abbotsbury, and it may be easier to follow the road to Langton Herring. From there the Path runs through a lovely valley to Chesil Beach and the Fleet, the stretch of water trapped behind it. The Path twists and turns to skirt the army ranges at Chickerell before crossing the ferry bridge at Portland Harbour and entering Weymouth, the last of the major resorts on the Path.

Weymouth to Lulworth Cove
13 miles

The Path starts again a mile east of the dramatic harbour. There is some pleasant cliff walking around Redcliffe Point and Black Head and on down to Osmington Mills, where the inland and coastal paths converge.

From Osmington Mills the Path runs along low cliffs and skirts a military radio station. Then it climbs inland to the top of the superb Ringstead Bay cliffs and heads towards the distinctive White Nothe. There now comes The Warren, a magnificent section of headlands and hollows with splendid seascapes. The Path runs sharply defined past Bat's Head and Durdle Door, a majestic rock archway. Now the walker descends to Lulworth Bay, an almost perfect circle hemmed in by cliffs save for a narrow outlet. The village and harbour are delightful, despite the countless thousands of summer visitors.

Lulworth to Kimmeridge
6 miles

There are extensive army ranges on the next stretch, and if firing is in progress a long detour through the lanes is obligatory. With luck all will be quiet, for the Path is strikingly beautiful and understandably not much walked. In any case there is little danger, for barriers, red flags and sentries guard all the routes to the artillery ranges. At the eastern end of Worbarrow Bay the walker reaches Kimmeridge, a tiny village with a post office-cum-shop and a short length of toll road leading to the foreshore.

Kimmeridge to Swanage
11 miles

From Kimmeridge the Path winds up past a 200-year-old folly, said to have been built for the ladies of nearby Smedmore Manor. This next section along the Kimmeridge Ledges to St Alban's Head must be one of the most dramatic in the entire country. The well-trodden Path hugs the great fissured cliffs and involves a number of fierce ups and downs, though in some places there are high-level detour tracks.

Chapman's Pool is a jewel, scooped in the shoulder of St Alban's Head. At the tip of the Head is a chapel, a stark and simple stone building that has withstood the gales of nearly a thousand years.

Between here and Durlston Head are some marvellous high spots–East Man, Dancing Ledge, Tilly Whim Caves and Great Globe. At Peveril Point, beyond the Durlston Country Park, the landscape begins to soften, Swanage Bay curving away from the full force of the westerlies. The Path breaks for the last time on the outskirts of the town.

Still a compact and pleasant resort, Swanage has some fascinating corners, especially in the old town. Here there is a tiny lock-up, a thirteenth-century clock tower and a group of mill-pond cottages. Surrounded by white cliffs and sandy bays, the town lies in the so-called Isle of Purbeck, a wide region of heath, woodland and grassy downs that has in fact always been part of the mainland.

Swanage to South Haven Point
7 miles

The final stretch of the Path starts at New Swanage and gently climbs the Purbeck Hills to the distinctive Old Harry rocks at Handfast Point. After Studland, another charming hamlet, there are a couple of miles of foreshore walking close to the lapping waves of Studland Bay before the ferry at South Haven Point is reached. Across the narrow neck of Poole Harbour lies the built-up waterfront of Sandbanks, with Poole and Bournemouth in the background.

Above right Durdle Door, a magnificent natural archway of Purbeck limestone.

Right Lyme Regis, a busy port since the Middle Ages and one of the earliest seaside resorts, beloved by holidaymakers since the eighteenth century.

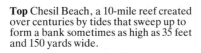

Top Chesil Beach, a 10-mile reef created over centuries by tides that sweep up to form a bank sometimes as high as 35 feet and 150 yards wide.

Above The wide expanse of Poole Harbour. South Haven Point, on the south-western side of the harbour entrance, is one end of England's longest long-distance path.

The Cleveland Way

Officially opened 1969
Length: approximately 100 miles
Going: hard

Ordnance Survey maps: 86, 93, 94 and 101

The Cleveland Way, which runs horseshoe-shaped from Helmsley in the North Yorkshire Moors to meet the coast at Saltburn and then south to Filey, is virtually two paths in one. The western half provides exhilarating walking across high moorland, while the eastern section follows one of Britain's wildest and most majestic coastlines. Because the entire route keeps fairly faithfully to the edge of the North York Moors National Park, civilization–in the form of towns and villages, accommodation and public transport–is never too far off.

It is this feature that makes the Cleveland Way a first-rate introduction to high-level distance walking. A word of warning, however, to those unused to hill-walking, especially the northern variety: the Way is tough going in places–very tough in a few–and neither its country nor its climate should ever be underestimated. If the elements turn sour it can test the mettle of the most determined walker.

Helmsley to Kilburn
12 miles

Long-term parking should not be difficult to arrange in Helmsley, but try the outskirts rather than the centre, which is a popular tourist target in summer. There is plenty of accommodation in the town, including a youth hostel. The chief attraction here, apart from the ruins of the Norman castle, is Rievaulx Abbey, just west of the town and north of the Cleveland Way. Rievaulx (pronounced 'Rivvis' locally) was founded in 1131 by Cistercian monks; the principal remains are a cruciform church, a magnificent example of the Early English style, and the refectory.

The Way starts from the Market Square. After the more or less obligatory diversion to the Abbey, flex your muscles, for the woodland path ascends immediately, rising quite sheer above the river Wye and winding tortuously among the limestone clefts and outcrops. Some fine panoramas

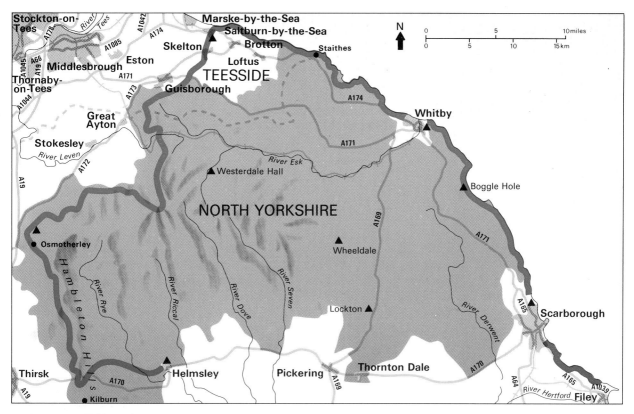

Left The square at Helmsley, starting-point of the Cleveland Way. Walkers may also choose a southward route, for the town is at one end of the Ebor Way (see page 157), which runs across the Vale of York, passing through the magnificent city, to Ilkley in the Dales.

Opposite The ruins of Rievaulx Abbey, a short distance north of the Way, the first Cistercian foundation in the north of England and one of many magnificent Norman churches in the region.

Top Helmsley Castle, thought to have been built in the twelfth century by Walter l'Espec, who also founded Rievaulx Abbey. The castle, which is defended by a double ditch, remained a residence until about 1700.

Above Gormire Lake and the Hambleton Hills, along the ridge of which the Way runs.

are the reward along this stretch, where Wordsworth once walked. The path continues through forestry plantations between Nettle Dale and Flassen Dale, and there is a short stretch of hard going before you reach the lane that takes you into the aptly-named Cold Kirby, a tiny, remote moorland settlement that must suffer more than its fair share of wind and weather in winter.

Now you have broken out on to the tops at last, leaving the lush valleys behind, and if the wind pipes up and the clouds start scudding you will discover how raw the northern climate can be.

It is exhilarating walking none the less, and after you have passed Hambleton House (the home base of the gliders you may have watched wheeling above) the views are

magnificent. At Sutton Bank, where some immense primordial eruption has left a sheer scarp as dramatic as any in Britain, you are quite suddenly confronted with birds-eye views over glittering Gormire Lake and the ribbon of road to Thirsk far below, Hood Hill jutting out like an island from a solid lowland sea. The Way continues along the Hambleton Ridge to an excellent National Park Information Centre complete with a display gallery, useful publications about the Park and a welcome café, while a detour path leads south to Roulston Scar. From here the views right across the Vale of York are even more majestic. Here, too, is the elongated White Horse above Kilburn, cut in the 1850s and covered with lime to make it stand out.

Roulston Scar seen from Sutton Bank, one of many exhilarating, wide views on the walk.

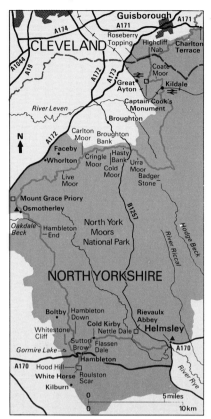

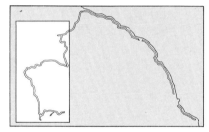

Above right Mount Grace Priory near Osmotherley, founded by Thomas Holland, Duke of Surrey. The monks' cells lead off the cloisters.

Right The line of the Hambleton Hills near Osmotherley.

Kilburn to Osmotherley
14 miles

The Way now follows Sutton Brow and Whitestone Cliff northwards, along some really precipitous edges, where especial care should be taken. This is the start of a longish 14-mile leg to Osmotherley along the western rim of the wild Hambleton Hills. Beyond the ancient hill-fort at Boltby Scar is Paradise Farm, where the path meets the old Hambleton Drove Road. Cattle were once driven along this ancient trackway from as far away as Scotland to the markets of central England.

Wide gorse-covered moors follow in quick succession now. If this seems like a tough uphill slog, remember that the highest point of the Drove Road is some 1200 feet. It is wild country indeed, despite the scattering of man-made forests and the slim finger of the television mast on the summit of Blisdale Moor. There are more splendid views as you begin to descend Hambleton End on a rough, sometimes steep track that eventually joins Oakdale Beck and continues into Osmotherley.

Though it has suffered from some modern housing, the village centre is still old. There is bed-and-breakfast and pub accommodation, with camping facilities nearby. Osmotherley is also the starting-point of the quaintly-named Lyke Wake Walk, which traces a straight line, more or less, right across the moors to Ravenscar and the coast 40 miles away. Those who complete this 24-hour pedestrian endurance test are awarded a coffin badge, and you have to be very fit to win it.

Osmotherley to Broughton
12 miles

The Way ascends again as soon as you leave Osmotherley, heading towards the ruins of Mount Grace Priory, a Carthusian monastery founded at the end of the fourteenth century. Above it, at an altitude of nearly 1000 feet, you join the Lyke Wake route, which may well be quite busy with walkers, especially during summer weekends. For the dozen miles or so over which the two paths coincide the Way is very well defined.

Now comes some of the best and the worst of the Cleveland Way, scenically speaking. In some places views are magnificent and romantic, in others (and much depends on the weather, of course) they are depressing and downright bleak, with numerous scars

and other long-abandoned industrial debris. The route is never dull, though, as it climbs and falls repeatedly across Live Moor, Carlton Moor–where there is another gliding club–and thence up to the great plateau of Cringle Moor some 1400 feet above sea level. Again, care is needed on some sections, particularly where the path meanders disconcertingly close to the scarp edges.

Cold Moor is partially relieved by forestry plantations, and Hasty Bank provides more fine views for the eye. The B1257 crosses the path here, a tempting escape route if you have had your fill of high-moor walking, at least for the time being.

Broughton to Guisborough 14 miles

The next stretch, Urra Moor, has the distinction of being, at 1500 feet, the highest along the Way. You may well be able to lean on the wind here, which with luck will be a following one, hastening you past the summit cairn and the massive Badger Stone above Hodge Beck. Here the Cleveland Way and the Lyke Wake route part company, the former turning north from the old Rosedale Ironstone Railway.

The gradual descent to the friendlier, wooded countryside around Kildale makes a pleasant contrast, while a backward glance or two should boost your ego considerably. A rest in the hamlet of Kildale will be well earned. There is a post office and a small shop but, alas, no pub.

From Kildale the path climbs up again on to Easby Moor and to a choice of routes northwards. Most walkers opt for the path along the ridge of Coate Moor, which takes them to the granite needle monument to Captain Cook, the 'Celebrated Circumnavigator' as the inscription puts it. A forestry track and minor lanes lead from here down to Great Ayton. This is something of a detour but worth it, for there is a pub and a shop selling home-baked bread, not to mention the tiny schoolhouse where the great explorer gained his early education.

If you want to take a day off, Great Ayton is a good place to do it, for nearby, and just a short detour from the main Cleveland Way, is Roseberry Topping, known locally, and with some accuracy, as Cleveland's Little Matterhorn. It rises to over 1000 feet, and those who like climbing may well be tempted to scale it, for the peak has dominated the horizon persistently.

The main path passes east of this singular landmark and heads for the impressive Highcliff Nab, thence skirting Guisborough, a mellow old market town with modern facilities and the remains of a twelfth-century priory.

Above The path near Osmotherley. For some dozen miles from the village to Hodge Beck the Cleveland Way and the Lyke Wake Walk (see page 158) follow the same route; they meet again on the coast at Ravenscar.

Top right The Way on the descent to Great Ayton from Captain Cook's monument on Easby Moor. In Great Ayton the explorer is commemorated again, in the form of an obelisk of rock from Point Hicks, the first Australian landfall seen by Cook.

Centre Roseberry Topping, 1057 feet high, visible for miles around a target for walkers and climbers.

Right Saltburn, where the Way forsakes the high moorland for equally dramatic cliff-walking.

Guisborough to Saltburn
8 miles

At the village of Charlton Terrace the path crosses the A171 and for a short while runs outside the National Park. There is no real excess of built-up area; despite the old shale tips and other mining debris, and the proximity of industrial Teesside a few miles northwest, it remains quite countryfied and pleasant. Route-finding can be confusing among the old mine workings, but the Way is well defined after Skelton. There is a little more up and down walking, mostly down, past a mill pond and under a viaduct, and then a pleasant woodland stretch concludes the inland section of the path as you reach Saltburn and the shoreline of the North Sea. Now your navigational problems are more or less over; all you have to do is to keep the sea on your left.

This is not to say that the route is easy from here on. There are some high ups and downs, and the path is as dramatic (and tricky in some places) as any in these islands. Do not get too near the edges; nor should you walk along the shore unless you are absolutely certain about the tides.

Before setting off again, enjoy a break in this pleasant little resort, where the ostentatious nineteenth-century high-rise hotels tower above the tiny beach. The Ship Inn welcomes Cleveland Way walkers and finding accommodation will not be difficult.

Saltburn to Staithes
8 miles

The first ascent from sea level is to the heights of the beautiful bay, a notorious spot for shipwrecks, via Hunt Cliff and past the remains of a Roman signal station. You will quickly understand the words of caution about watching your step, especially if the surf is thundering far below.

A swooping descent to sea level again brings you to Skinningrove. This is a strangely evocative place, a derelict bygone of the industrial revolution, once pulsating with iron foundries and blast furnaces, for it was here that ironstone was discovered in the mid-nineteenth century. Yet time has brought a kind of dignity that is both sad and mystifying. The village is compact and confined almost entirely within a narrow gorge of majestic natural cliffs. It is suddenly come upon and as quickly left behind.

The sheer exhilaration of this lofty cliff-path, which continues more or less unbroken to Scarborough, is better experienced than described. As a beginning, you could hardly wish for anything more dramatic than Boulby Cliff which, at 660 feet, is the highest coastal point in all England. It is splendidly regal too, despite the heavy scarring of old alum workings. Today, however, the plundered landscape has been softened and as at Skinningrove it provides a fascinating glimpse of recent industrial archaeology.

Staithes, too, is almost a fragment of the living past, a tight-knit seafaring

The coast at Whitby. The coastal section of the Way is varied and exciting, windy high stretches interspersed with secluded harbours and inlets.

community which has only recently discarded the celebrated Staithes Bonnets and where the coble work-boats are still launched for fishing rather than for tourism. There is accommodation here, a fine waterfront pub and a little camping-ground, all snuggling in a steep and narrow ravine.

The young Captain Cook worked here, by the way, as a grocer's boy.

Staithes to Whitby
12 miles

The path now climbs steeply, at first following the cliff edge, then turning inland to round Penny Nab and pass

Hinderwell. At Runswick, once a fishing village like Staithes but now full of holiday chalets, it drops to sea level and a beach walk before ascending yet again to the headland of Kettleness. This massive promontory was heavily exploited for its alum deposits but none the less remains magnificent scenically, with views all the way to Whitby. There is an interesting Roman fort near Goldsborough where some grisly remains of Roman murder were found by archaeologists excavating the site just after the First World War. From the aptly-named Sandsend you have to walk along roads for the final couple of miles into Whitby, though if your luck is in the tide will be out and you can go along the beach, which is far nicer.

Whitby must be one of the most beautiful ports in the world. Its location, as far as mariners are concerned, is perfect, a deep-water harbour sheltered from all but the northerly wind. Every aspect delights the eye, the riot of colour-washed houses clinging to the steep banks of the river Esk, which cuts the town almost exactly in half. Cook lived here, and in the yards his two famous ships, *Endeavour* and *Resolution*, were built. The seamen's church is reached via the 199 steps (part in fact of the Cleveland Way), which also lead to the dramatic ruined abbey, in what must be one of the most exposed locations in Christendom. The museum has a particularly fine collection of fossils, and the port area is always a friendly bustle of activity. There is a youth hostel here as well as every other kind of accommodation and a choice of camping sites seaward from Hawsker, a couple of miles further along the coast *en route* to Robin Hood's Bay.

Above The tiny alleyways of Staithes, still a genuine fishing village despite increasing tourism.

Above right The harbour at Whitby.

Right The ruins of Whitby Abbey, built in the thirteenth century on a headland above the town. The first abbey here was constructed in AD 657, six years before the Synod of Whitby, at which the English churches accepted the authority of Rome.

Whitby to Robin Hood's Bay
8 miles

There is yet another lovely stretch of cliff-walking beyond Whitby towards Robin Hood's Bay. This huddle of houses and tiny harbour looks for all the world like a smuggler's haunt, which indeed it was. For the walker it is still a delight to explore, and he may well find himself a trace smug as he watches motorists being turned away for lack of parking space. Robin Hood's Bay is sorely pressed by tourists, but some of the old charm remains.

Robin Hood's Bay to Scarborough
14 miles

The walker is soon striking out across another splendid and virtually unpopulated curve of coast. The path here roller-coasts between sea level and 600

feet and some care is needed where route kisses the edges. At the delightfully-named Boggle Hole there is a youth hostel and at Ravenscar, where the Lyke Wake Walk finishes in a suitably dramatic fashion, a hotel. There are regal views from here back around the bay.

At Hayburn Wyke you drop down steeply from the cliff edge path to one of the prettiest—and least discovered—coves along this stretch of coast. From Cloughton Wyke, another distinctive boulder-strewn inlet, the going becomes more gentle as you approach Scarborough.

Britain's first spa resort and still stamped with solid nineteenth-century opulence, Scarborough is one of the biggest and busiest seaside towns in the country. The castle with its Norman

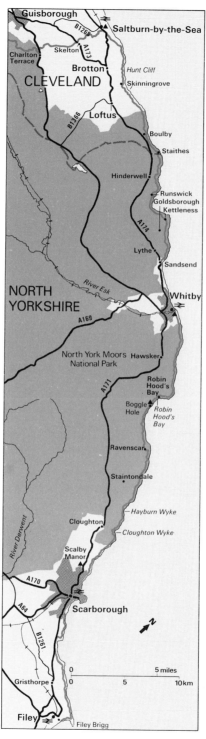

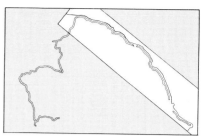

Above left Robin Hood's Bay, at the northern tip of the great, 3-mile-long inlet.

Left Scarborough old town and, on the headland, the remnants of the twelfth-century castle.

Ravenscar, at the southern end of Robin Hood's Bay. A hotel has been built where a Roman lighthouse once stood.

keep is worth seeing, and the promenades still retain the flavour of a more gracious age, even though development is almost suffocating. There is a choice of camping grounds near Scalby Manor and also a youth hostel.

Scarborough to Filey
8 miles

South of the town, the Way may well prove somewhat disappointing to those who have tackled the grander sections further north. The bays with their relatively low cliffs are pleasant enough, but you do have to run the gauntlet of a succession of holiday developments of one kind or another.

The one feature that stops the path ending with a whimper is Filey Brigg. Here the dark rock thrusts massively and dramatically seawards, a magnificent sight when the surf is running. On a clear day there will be marvellous views over Filey town some two miles away and across to Flamborough Head.

An extension of the Cleveland Way – to be known as the Wolds Way – south from Filey is planned. It will run along the chalk hills of the Yorkshire Wolds, through farming country and across some of the prettiest of the Dales to finish at North Ferriby, near Hull.

Filey harbour and, in the background, the Brigg, end point of the Cleveland Way.

The Pembrokeshire Coast Path

Officially opened 1970

The first designated long-distance footpath in Wales

Length: 168 miles
Going: hard/medium

Ordnance Survey maps: 145, 157 and 158

This Path offers splendid coastal walking for virtually its whole length. Although it is entirely within the Pembrokeshire Coast National Park, and much of it runs through wild and sparsely populated country, accommodation is available at reasonable intervals. The southern starting-point is at Amroth, just west of Pendine Sands on the shores of Carmarthen Bay. The northern end is at St Dogmaels, a tiny suburb of Cardigan, which is itself hardly more than a fair-sized market town. In between there are just three towns of any size, Tenby, Pembroke and Fishguard. This is essentially a country walk, then, and those intent on completing all 168 miles

(more like 200 if you include the ups and downs of the landscape) usually start at the southern end and travel clockwise around the peninsula.

Curiously, though one must penetrate deep into west Wales to reach the start of the Path, the region hereabouts is less, rather than more, Welsh. The reason for this goes back nine hundred years to the Norman Conquest. This small corner was the only part of the Principality where the Normans met little or no resistance (they reached Pembroke as early as 1090), and they settled here in some numbers, bringing Flemish migrants with them to work the land. The area has kept its separate identity ever since, and the English atmosphere, especially noticeable in Tenby, is reinforced by the invasion of English holidaymakers, an annual event since Victorian times. Nowadays, a high percentage of these visitors are campers and caravanners.

The harbour at Tenby, a popular resort close to the start of the Path.

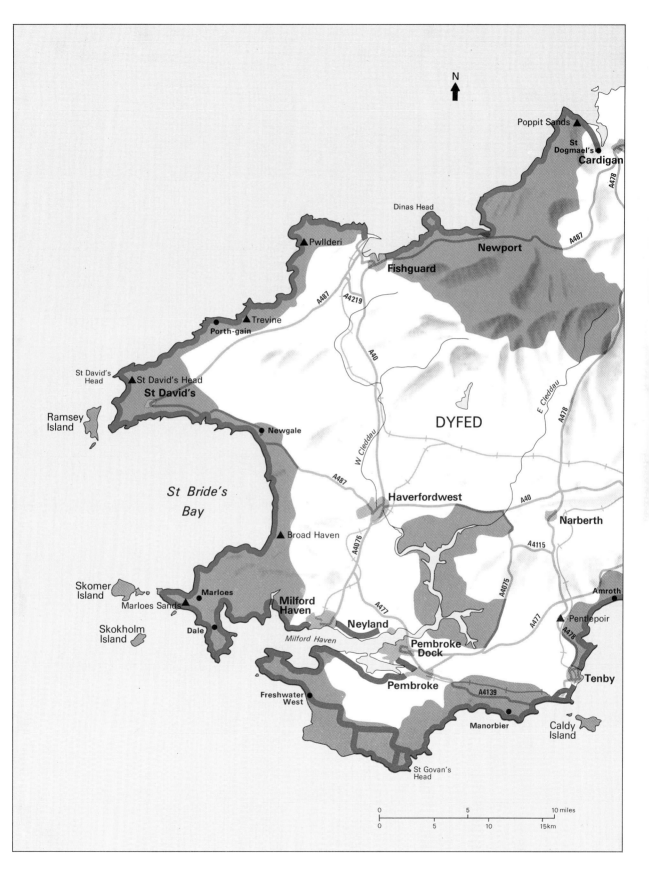

N

Poppit Sands ▲
St Dogmael's ●
Cardigan
A478

Dinas Head

▲Pwllderi

Newport

Fishguard

A487

A4219

A40

● Porth-gain ▲Trevine

St David's Head

▲St David's Head
St David's

Ramsey Island

● Newgale

DYFED

E Cleddau

A478

St Bride's Bay

W Cleddau

A487

A4076

▲ Broad Haven

Haverfordwest

A40

Narberth

A4115

A4075

Skomer Island

Marloes Sands ▲ **Marloes**

Milford Haven

Amroth ●

Skokholm Island

Dale ●

Neyland

A477

▲ Pentlepoir

A478

Freshwater West ●

Milford Haven

Pembroke Dock

Pembroke

A4139

Tenby

Manorbier ●

Caldy Island

St Govan's Head

| 0 | | 5 | | 10 miles |
| 0 | 5 | | 10 | 15km |

Amroth to Tenby
6 miles

As the pretty little hamlet of Amroth (where, incidentally, long-term parking should not be difficult to arrange) is left behind, the walker's leg muscles are stretched immediately, for the Path at once winds steeply upwards and continues largely as a roughish cliff-top route to Tenby. This stretch is a good half day's walk and is quite hard going in places, though it is reasonably well defined. You drop down to sea level and the road just before the curiously named village of Saunders-foot, which is modern, none too pretty (except for the harbour) and always very crowded in summer. Near Coppet Hall there was a large anthracite mine during the nineteenth century, and the Path runs through a tunnel used by the colliery tramway.

Highish cliffs and a fine seascape follow Saundersfoot with views across Tenby to Caldy Island and beyond. The going is rough on the approach to Waterwynch Bay, then easier into Tenby.

This may well be enough for the first day, especially if you are not yet in peak physical condition. In any case, Tenby

is a lovely old town, and it offers a wide range of accommodation. A call at the Tourist Information Office (open every day including Sundays in summer), at the northern end of the town, may prove useful.

Do allow yourself time to explore, for the town has much of interest within its fine thirteenth-century walls. Its history goes back well before the Normans (it was a stronghold of the Welsh as early as the ninth century), and there is an interesting museum, a superb promenade and a silver-sand North Beach as inviting as any in the country. It is a relief too to arrive on foot amid this maze of narrow streets, so frustrating for drivers and always crowded in summer. Any shopping for forgotten essentials should be done here, since the next town of any size near the Path is Pembroke, a long way ahead. South of the town, Kiln Caravan and Camping Park has a large, level area for tents and up-to-date facilities.

Tenby to Manorbier
10 miles

It is easy going at first from Tenby, past the golf course and Penally, and then either to Lydstep around the inlet or via Giltar Point, which is scenic but a mile or so longer. Some road walking is required around Old Castle Head to skirt an army establishment. Back on the Path, above the well-preserved Norman remains of Manorbier Castle, you pass The King's Quoit, a Neolithic burial chamber dating from about 3000 BC. The Castle itself, its name, the terrain of heavily indented cliffs and indeed the very atmosphere are all strongly reminiscent of Brittany: a touch of France within an English enclave surrounded by a land and a people that could hardly be more Welsh.

Manorbier to Freshwater West
18 miles

Once away from the car park and picnic area you will have the coast path more or less to yourself again for the fairly easy, undulating walk to the wide sands of Freshwater East. There now follow some superb sections of limestone and red sandstone cliff, especially around the tiny harbour of Stackpole Quay and at the commanding height of Stackpole Head, where centuries of pounding seas have scoured out caves and arches at the waterline.

Ministry of Defence property means

Opposite above Tenby harbour and town. Despite its solidly English Victorian buildings, the splashes of vivid colour give the town a Riviera atmosphere.

Opposite below Manorbier Castle, one of the best examples of Norman architecture in South Wales and birthplace, in about 1146, of Giraldus Cambrensis, the celebrated Welsh topographer and historian.

Below centre Windswept St Govan's Head, one of many magnificent stretches along the Path.

Below The Green Bridge, a spectacular rock formation passed just as the Path turns inland to skirt the army firing ranges.

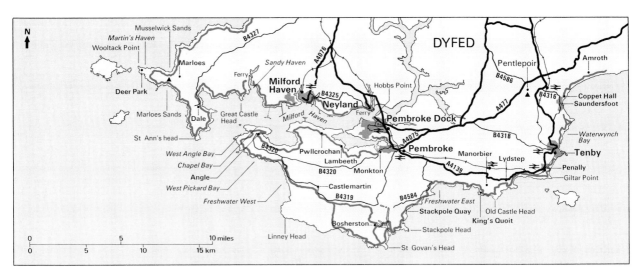

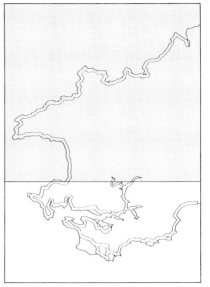

that you will have to detour inland at St Govan's Head if the ranges are operating and walk through Bosherston, Castlemartin and on to Freshwater West on the road. This is pleasant enough, but take the footpath between St Govan's Head and Stack Rocks if the red flags are not flying, if only to see the colonies of sea birds crowding the limestone ledges. There is no option but to go inland at the Stack Rocks and The Green Bridge, for the whole of Linney Head is a training-ground. From Castlemartin the road, albeit a quiet one, brings you to Freshwater West, where you rejoin the coast amid a sweep of sand dunes.

The tiny St Govan's Chapel, just 18 feet by 12, set in the cliffs below St Govan's Head.

Freshwater West to Pembroke 18 miles

The next section is rugged, lonely and hard going in places, derelict wartime equipment and installations dotting the landscape. There are some splendid cliffs, though care is needed in places where the path is crumbling. If you find the going too tough, take the minor road that runs roughly parallel a short distance inland.

There is an Iron Age fort (c. 300 BC) at West Pickard Bay, and at West Angle Bay, where the landing place is about the same age, ships would un-load copper from Ireland. Rat Island, just offshore at the southern end of the bay, is something of a misnomer, for its inhabitants are mostly gulls and the comparatively rare choughs. You can cut straight across the headland via the B4320 or take the purist's route around the promontory, where a number of forts were built in the nineteenth century, past Chapel Bay. Angle village has shops, pubs, a hotel and a camping-ground. Most walkers are happy to rest for a spell here after the tough but exciting walk around the wild and remote headland.

From here to Pembroke the pre-vailing westerly wind will be at your back and the views are a study in contrasts. Impressive and alien, Mil-ford Haven is a fascinating, concentrated huddle of commerce. The largest oil port in Britain, it is a perfect natural harbour and can accept tankers of 300,000 tons. Along the shore are refineries belonging to all the major oil companies. Indeed, the Path actually

Pembroke Castle, symbol of Norman dominion in Wales. The keep is 75 feet high, and the outer wall has seven bastion towers.

crosses part of the Texaco complex and skirts the oil-fired power station at Pwllcrochan. But the water-borne bustle and the shoreline industry are all carefully confined, and if you lift your eyes the rounded green hills still domi-nate. In fact, the Path is a pleasant one through woods and fields, especially after Lambeeth, past the medieval priory of Monkton and up to the very ramparts of Pembroke Castle.

Built on a bluff almost encircled by the river, the Castle, which has been a symbol of English influence since the eleventh century, is still very impress-ive, a tribute to the stonemason's art. Birthplace of Henry VII, partly des-

troyed by Cromwell's army, Pembroke Castle stands proud, dominating the pretty little town, which to this day has an English air.

Pembroke to Dale
18 miles

Take the Haven Road Bridge, which replaced the old ferry from Hobbs Point in 1975, out of Pembroke and across the harbour into Neyland. The Path starts again at Hazel beach and continues westwards along Milford Haven and into Wales, but first it passes a complex of oil refineries and, frankly, if you can avoid this section so much the better. Two miles or so to the

west, you will reach Sandy Haven, where at low tide you can cross the causeway (unfortunately there is no alternative route at high tide).

There is pleasant, wooded scenery here at first, followed by impressive rock cliffs past Great Castle Head and then some mud flats along the shoreline between Musselwick and Dale. Cross the Gann river at low water to avoid a long detour. At Dale, a popular sailing centre, there are shops, a pub and a post office.

Dale to Marloes
12 miles

If time is limited, you can cut straight

across from Dale to Westdale Bay. Walk out to St Ann's Head if you can, however, for the Path is good and the cliffs impressive. There is a youth hostel near Marloes Sands (a superb strand renowned for its lava, or edible seaweed), and accommodation in the village of Marloes a short walk inland.

Marloes to Newgale
19 miles

A fine Path takes you around Wooltack Point, a wild and exciting coast. The names of the two offshore islands, Skomer and Skokholm, remind us of the Viking presence here between the eighth and tenth centuries. Both are

now nature reserves, and Skomer may be visited by boat from Martin's Haven, just around the headland. Below the Deer Park (designed for deer, although they seem never to have been introduced) is Jack Sound, where you may be lucky enough to spot grey seals.

After passing along the cliff top, the Path follows the line of Musselwick Sands and then passes Nab Head. Between here and Little Haven there are sections of overgrown bracken and bramble followed by woodland. Beyond Little Haven the Path is better, but the scenery is less spectacular. Watch out for old mine workings as you approach Newgale, where it is perhaps more sensible to stick to the road.

There are pubs, shops and guest houses at Broad Haven, Nolton Haven and Newgale, for this is a recognized holiday coast not far from Haverfordwest. Broad Haven, which has a National Park Information Centre, marks the end of the west Pembroke coal seam—hence the mineworkings in this area. At Newgale there is something of a Welsh Chesil Bank, a long pebble pile built up by countless winter tides crashing into the west-facing storm beach. The sands in front form one of the best beaches along the whole Path. There is a pub near here and several camping-grounds nearby.

Above left Marloes Sands, a popular spot for summer holidaymakers. The bird sanctuary on Skokholm, the island lying offshore, was created before the Second World War and remains a centre of serious research: day-trippers are not allowed, and visitors must stay at least a week.

Top Newgale village and sands on the shore of St Bride's Bay.

St David's Cathedral and the ruins of the medieval Bishop's Palace. The tiny city has been a place of worship since the patron saint of Wales chose the site in the sixth century.

115

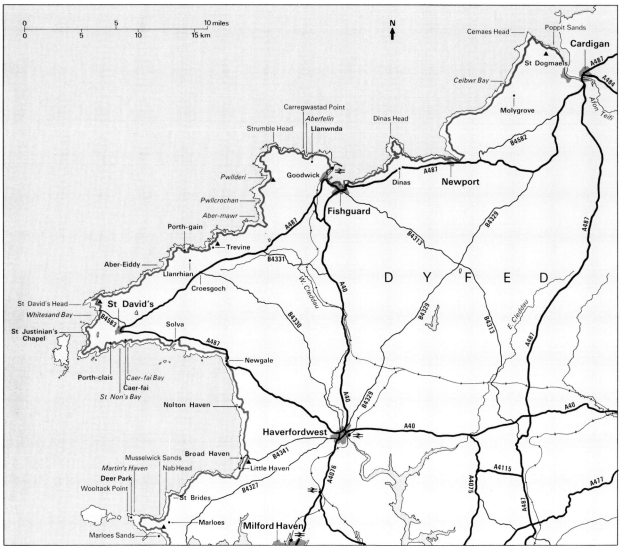

Newgale to Porth-clais
12 miles

High-level walking and some steep ups and downs over a well-defined and well-maintained path take you to Solva. The ancient land-locked harbour here, one of the prettiest in Wales, is a haven for small pleasure craft. The approach offers fine views, and there will be a fair degree of summer crowds when you get there, but not excessively so. There are also pubs, a café and shops.

The Path between Solva and Caer-fai Bay is eroded and overgrown in parts, but lanes and inland paths provide a pleasant enough alternative, especially in bad weather. Caer-fai is a popular holiday beach and the footpath from here right around to Whitesand Bay is well trodden and easy going,

with the exception of a few short stretches. This is a magnificent, really wild section where the coastline is populated only by seabirds. Ramsey Island, now a bird sanctuary, dominates the skyline offshore. Here you are far away from the workaday world, and even in high summer you should have it more or less to yourself.

At St Non's Bay (where it is said that St David was born in about 520 AD), you will surely temporarily forsake the coastal path and take the minor road leading to the famous cathedral city of St David's, the smallest in all Britain, hardly more than an overgrown village. The beautifully preserved twelfth-century cathedral, dedicated to the patron saint of Wales, lies almost hidden (as it was meant to be against marauding Viking ships) in a valley

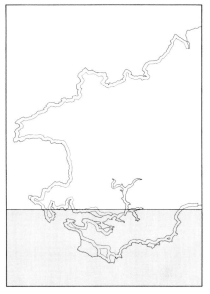

cleft, a gem of history not to be missed. The town has a choice of accommodation and shops, plus a choice of camping sites and a youth hostel at nearby Llaethdy.

Porth-clais to Porth-gain
8 miles

You can rejoin the Path at Porth-clais, a beautiful inlet that was once the busy supply port for St David's. There is fine walking now, as you hug the low cliffs along Ramsey Sound. Ancient forts and burial mounds and the Chapel of St Justinian punctuate the walk to Whitesand Bay.

There are some of the finest views of the whole walk from St David's Head, and the Path is quite easy all the way to Porth-gain. This is a good place for a rest, and there is a pub and a café tucked away beneath sheer cliffs. Inland, a mile from Croesgoch, there is a first-class touring site called Torbont, a good base for those who want to explore this splendid section at length.

Porth-gain to Strumble Head
14 miles

From Porth-gain the Path is rough, dangerous in places and not too well defined, and you might do better to take to farm tracks and lanes to Abermawr beach and then walk on to Pwllcrochan beach. The Path is still up and down here, but the going is easier. Between Pwllcrochan and Pwllderi, where there is a youth hostel, there is more superb scenery.

The next stretch is as remote as it is exhilarating to walk: stern, with majestic cliffs and crashing surf below, while hosts of seabirds wheel and turn above. The long haul around Strumble Head is rough going in places, though, and not for the novice or those out of condition.

Out at the point, the lighthouse-keeper will probably let you look around if there are not too many other visitors. The light itself was built in about 1908 and is kept in pristine condition.

Top The coast near Strumble Head, where a lighthouse warns ships of the treacherous shore.

Right Whitesand Bay (known in Welsh as Porthmawr), a large inlet near St David's.

Strumble Head to Fishguard
8 miles

There is more hard going round the headland, on which the Path is only vaguely defined in places. At Carregwastad a stone commemorates the 'invasion' by the French in 1797, when a motley force of some thousand irregulars landed with the intention of marching on Chester and Liverpool: it took just two days to capture them; most surrendered after taking women wearing red cloaks for militiamen.

The going is rough from here, along a heavily indented coastline, though things gradually become easier, and there are fine views over Fishguard Bay. A gradual descent to Harbour Village and Goodwick brings you first to a tarmac road and then to a footpath into old Fishguard.

Fishguard to Newport
12 miles

It is easier walking now across open cliff tops. The panoramas are splendid and there are attractive beaches and coves between Dinas Head and Newport Sands. The area is never crowded, though, despite the increasingly frequent coastal villages. At Dinas you can take a short cut across the base of the headland or keep to the cliff edge, much the more attractive alternative if you have time. Newport, where you make a short detour to cross the estuary bridge, has all the facilities the walker needs.

Newport to St Dogmaels
13 miles

Miles of really unspoiled coast follow next. The Path to Ceibwr Bay is well marked but hard going unless you pace yourself carefully. The only habitation around here is Moylegrove, half a mile or so inland, which has a post office and shop. There are fine crags, caves and jagged rock faces *en route,* seals below (if you are lucky) and a whole variety of seabirds above. The entire area is virtually undiscovered by holidaymakers, and you may well complete this stretch without seeing another person.

The route continues thus almost all the way to the lowish promontory of Cemaes Head. The Path itself is well defined and though the going is hard in places it is not too strenuous if you are reasonably fit. On its final leg, the Path descends to the wide golden sweep of Poppit Sands and the Teifi estuary and thence leads via a minor road into St Dogmaels.

Opposite The attractive harbour at
Fishguard. The bay is deep enough to
accommodate many ocean-going vessels.

Above Dinas Head, towards the northern
end of the Path. Walkers who take the short
cut and bypass the headland will miss one of
the most attractive parts of the entire route.

Right Newport, a tiny town on the estuary
of the river Nevern. Nearby are a number of
cromlech, ancient burial-chambers
consisting of upright stones surmounted by
a horizontal capstone.

The Pennine Way

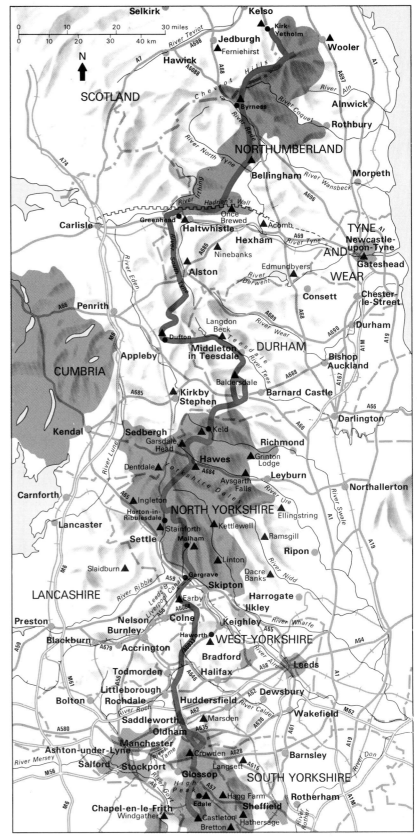

Officially opened 1965
Length: 250 miles
Going: severe/hard

Ordnance Survey maps: 74, 80, 86, 87, 91, 92, 98, 103, 109 and 110

The Pennine Way is the ultimate challenge. Eventually, every keen distance-walker will set his sights on tackling this marathon route along the backbone of England. And rightly so: from Edale in the Peak District, through the Yorkshire Dales and the Northumberland National Park to Kirk Yetholm, amid the Cheviots and just over the Scottish border, the walker is surrounded by a landscape that is always rugged, often majestic, sometimes breathtaking.

The Way is not a challenge to be accepted lightly. It offers some of the roughest walking in the country. Much of the path winds across featureless peat moors, often miles from the nearest habitation. There are boggy stretches that leave boots wet for hours on end, steep river-bed tracks where you have to pick your way across rocks and boulders, and vast tracts of heather. Above all, there are the great windswept peaks that thrust skywards 2000 feet or more at regular intervals along the route. Kinder Scout,

Bleaklow, Pen-y-Ghent, Great Shunner Fell, Cross Fell and the Cheviots all demand the utmost respect.

That only experienced walkers, competent with map and compass, should attempt the route, or even a small part of it, goes without saying. In good weather they will meet no major problems. In adverse conditions, the going can be beyond the endurance of even the toughest and best-prepared.

The man who, virtually alone, was responsible for the creation of the Pennine Way is Tom Stephenson, the first secretary of the Ramblers' Association. All of us who walk for leisure owe a great debt of gratitude to him. It was he who, in 1935, first put forward the idea of the long-distance path, at that time no more than a visionary's dream. It was he and his association who fought doggedly against formidable opposition from both government and private interests for the public's right of access to the countryside. The battle lasted for thirty years, until, on 24 April 1965, before a crowd of 2000 enthusiasts on Malham Moor, the whole of the route was officially opened, the first designated long-distance route in the country. At that moment a priceless privilege was won, the right to shoulder a pack and don a pair of walking boots and wander not only over the Pennine Way but also over the host of other routes created in its wake.

Lose Hill seen from Mam Tor, near the southern end of the Pennine Way, forerunner of the tough terrain along Britain's most strenuous and, some would say, most romantic long-distance path.

Edale to Crowden
15 miles

The approach to Edale and the start of the Pennine Way from the Chapel-en-le-Frith road is marvellous. As you top the summit of Mam Tor the full beauty of the valley is revealed: a huge natural amphitheatre, Edale nestling at the bottom and the towering, rugged plateau of Kinder Scout rising almost sheer to the north. There is only one way to see this high, wide country–on foot.

Edale itself is a busy bustle of walkers during the holiday season and at most weekends. The village has a couple of pubs and a selection of camping-grounds, but otherwise accommodation is limited. There is a car-park, a railway station and an information centre. Hope, a few miles away on the main road, is a popular alternative base.

The walker has a choice of paths right away. The first of the three wet-weather loops along the Way winds around the great plateau, via Upper Booth, Jacobs Ladder and Edale Cross, to join the main route at Kinder Downfall. Take this path only if you must, for the classic start, from the northern end of the village, is the assault on Grindsbrook and Kinder Scout.

Green and friendly at first, and made almost motorway-wide by the countless feet that have tramped it, the path soon becomes rougher and boulder-strewn as the deep clough bites into the sheer hillside. Some care must be taken when crossing the frequent streams, for the start of the day is no time to ship a bootful of water. Near the top, amid loose scree and huge boulders, the path becomes for the only time in its entire length almost a climb. There are no sheer drops, however, and no more than a steadying hand will be necessary to gain the lip of the plateau, nearly 2000 feet high.

Top Withins, one of the familiar landmarks in the Peak District. Tackling such summits provides good practice for the rigours of the Way.

Gaze down now on the other walkers labouring far below before you turn to face the world of peat ahead, a sombre, brown-black desert of hummocks and coarse grass tufts crossed by numerous channels, many 10 feet deep or more. The land is sometimes firm under foot; more often it is black, oozing sludge where delicate steps are necessary to keep the feet dry.

The path across this barren, wind-swept tract is only vaguely defined until you reach Kinder Downfall, and you will have to consult map and compass at frequent intervals. When the stream that feeds Kinder reservoir to the east is in spate, the plunging waterfall is spectacular. The loop joins the main route here, and the Way is clearly defined for the next step along Black

Left Kinder Scout, first of many exhilarating ascents along the Way.

Below The Calder valley, wild and remote, yet barely more than a few miles from some of the country's oldest and grimmest industrial landscapes.

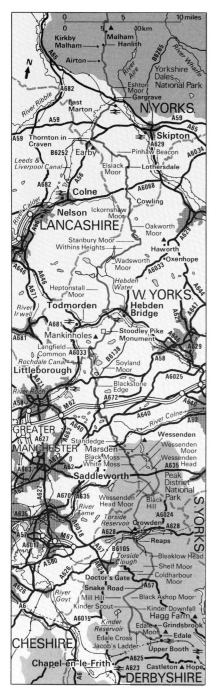

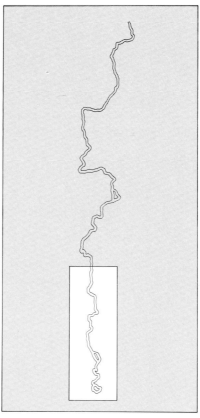

Heptonstall, an ancient weavers' village set high in the moors above Hebden Bridge.

Crowden to Standedge
12 miles

There is a steep ascent from here on to more wild and windswept tops. Black Hill and Wessenden Head Moor are only a little less dramatic than Kinder and Bleaklow. The second wet-weather loop runs through Wessenden Valley alongside Wessenden reservoir, and you may prefer this to the peat path over the summit. The path now strikes north-west across White Moss and Black Moss, which are again heavy going in wet weather, to Standedge and the A62.

Standedge to Haworth
22 miles

It is easier going to the M62, which is crossed by a pleasant footbridge. The majestic gritstone crags of Blackstone Edge follow, and the path passes the distinctive Stoodley Pike monument commemorating the battle of Waterloo before gradually descending to the Calder valley.

Ashop Moor to Mill Hill, then on to cross the A57.

You cross the old Roman Road at Doctor's Gate and immediately begin to tackle Bleaklow Head, which, if anything, is even sterner than Kinder Scout. It is hard walking across more peat until Torside Clough is reached. From here it is downhill more or less all the way to Reaps, Torside reservoir and Crowden.

Above Malham Dale, its green a brief, refreshing contrast with the windswept tops behind and in front.

Right Malham Cove, 250 feet of sheer limestone cliff formed in the Ice Age. Above the cave is the famous Malham Pavement, a series of fissured limestone blocks that rainfall is continually widening.

The Way now crosses Heptonstall Moor past Hebden Water in gentler country dotted with dry-stone walls and ascends to Withins Heights, supposedly the Wuthering Heights of Emily Bronte's novel. Haworth and the famous parsonage, the childhood home of the three sisters, lie about three miles to the east.

Haworth to Gargrave
16 miles

Past Cowling and Lothersdale, there are splendid views from Pinhaw Beacon before the descent to Thornton in Craven on the A56. North of here, the Way follows the towpath alongside the Leeds and Liverpool Canal a short way, before crossing pleasant fields and entering Gargrave village, which straddles the main road from Skipton to Settle.

Above The brooding summit of Pen-y-Ghent, one of the most spectacular peaks along the Way. With nearby Ingleborough and Whernside it forms the famous Three Peaks, tackled regularly by climbers and fell-runners.

Left Hardrow Force, a short way north of Hawes. The water here drops 100 feet, the highest unbroken fall in the country.

Here you are at the gateway to the North Yorkshire Moors, and both the terrain and atmosphere undergo a tangible change. The long miles of peat moor, the urban encroachment and the noisy main roads are left behind. From here on you travel through open country dotted with small townships, still much as it was a century ago, a secret Britain unwinding to the Scottish border and beyond.

Gargrave to Malham
10 miles

Leaving the banks of the pretty river Aire behind, you enter the Yorkshire Dales National Park and follow the path across Eshton Moor, past Airton and on to Malham. Lush Malham Dale is indeed a tranquil contrast with the high, windswept and sometimes bleak terrain behind. Here the greens are

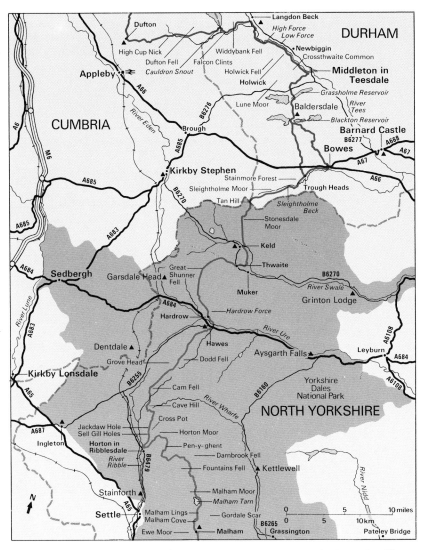

Opposite top The lonely village of Thwaite huddling beneath Great Shunner Fell, the soothing grey of its stones providing a welcome relief from the wild landscape all around.

Opposite Market day at Hawes, 850 feet high amid the fells.

more vivid, the climate softer and more friendly, and snuggling villages invite the walker to rest and recuperation.

Malham village has a helpful information centre, a store, café and a couple of welcome pubs. There is also a youth hostel nearby and a choice of farm camping-grounds. Malham is mentioned in Domesday Book, and there are some old buildings, including the Lister Arms pub. Ducks waddle the main street and there is a charming hump-back bridge.

Malham to Horton
16 miles

From Gordale Scar east of the village, a towering canyon 400 feet high, the Pennine Way may be rejoined at Malham Tarn. All along this stretch the exposed limestone crags create a backdrop of dramatic beauty. Malham

Cove, less than a mile from the village, is another natural amphitheatre, its main cliff face nearly 250 feet high.

An ancient pack-horse trail is followed now as the walker gradually climbs to the summit of Fountains Fell and marches on across splendid open moorland towards the summit of Pen-y-Ghent, the most celebrated of all the peaks the Pennine Way passes. Although not the highest along the Way (Cross Fell has that distinction), it is nevertheless the most glamorous and in some lights really does seem like a crouching animal. You now realize from what the Golden Lion, the village inn far below in Horton in Ribblesdale, takes its name.

Horton to Hawes
15 miles

Pot-holing is a popular pursuit around

here, and a couple of miles beyond Horton you pass Sell Gill Holes, Cross Pot and Jackdaw Hole. From Cave Hill the track is well defined, running in more or less a straight line across Cam Fell and Dodd Fell, about 1800 feet high, to Hawes, in the green valley of Wensleydale.

Hawes, where one of England's most important sheep markets is held, is a delightful township of gritstone houses and narrow, winding streets, famous for its tangy Wensleydale cheese. There is a good choice of accommodation here, including a youth hostel.

Hawes to Keld
14 miles

Crossing the valley, the Path skirts the hamlet of Hardrow, where it is almost a point of honour to pass through the Green Dragon Inn to view the cele-

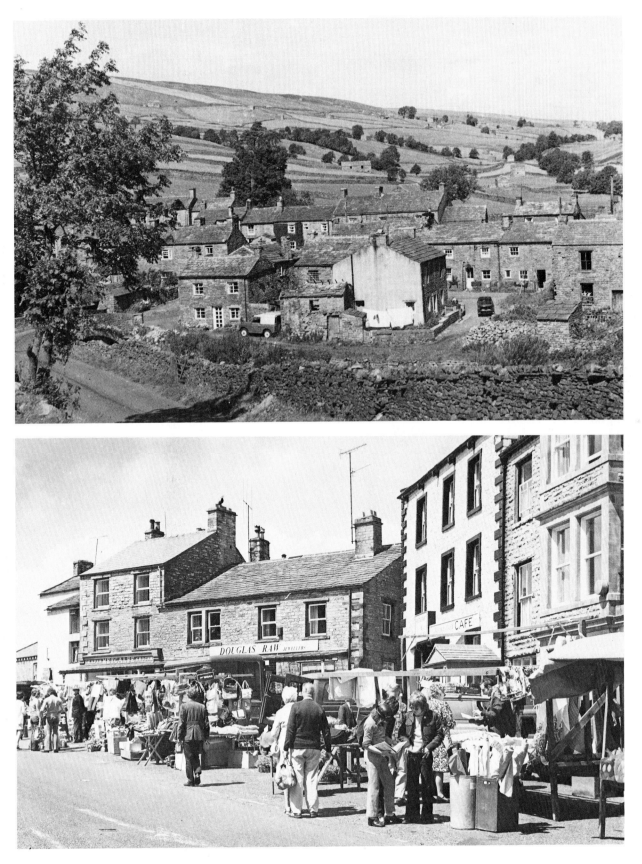

brated Hardrow Force. This is the highest unbroken cataract fall in Great Britain, a clear drop of 100 feet. Described by Wordsworth and painted by Turner, the waterfall is part of a mini-canyon, in formation rather like those of Arizona.

Now it is high country again across the wide expanse of Great Shunner Fell with fine views over Swaledale ahead. The summit cairn of Shunner seems an unconscionable time coming, but the going is good and the route well marked. There is accommodation at Thwaite, a mellow and picturesque village, and a youth hostel near Keld further up the valley. Buttertubs, a steep and spectacular ravine a couple of miles south of Thwaite, is a famous beauty spot. There are camping-grounds at nearby Muker and just north of Keld (which has no pub).

Keld to Middleton
19 miles

For an elevated pint you must continue north to the summit of Tan Hill, where you will find the highest (and most isolated) pub in England, a warm and welcome oasis. The main route now runs for about 20 miles across some really wild country to Middleton in Teesdale, and there is little or no accommodation on the way. Stainmore is open and desolate and demands a hard day's walking. Most walkers therefore choose the third and final loop, which veers east from Trough Heads and follows Sleightholme Beck to Bowes, an historic little town with a massive and fascinating museum, plus good accommodation. Leaving Bowes the loop path crosses the moor and joins the direct route at the head of Blackton reservoir. From here the Way continues to Middleton, where once more the walker finds himself in a beautiful, green and friendly valley.

Right The Way near Middleton in Teesdale, for two hundred years the centre of a busy lead-mining industry but now no more than a pleasant backwater.

Opposite top The highest, remotest and most welcome pub in England, 1758 feet high atop Tan Hill.

Opposite centre Cauldron Snout, where the river Tees falls 1000 feet in a succession of cascades.

Opposite bottom Dufton, an isolated village astride the Way halfway between Middleton and Alston and a pleasant place in which to relax and regain strength.

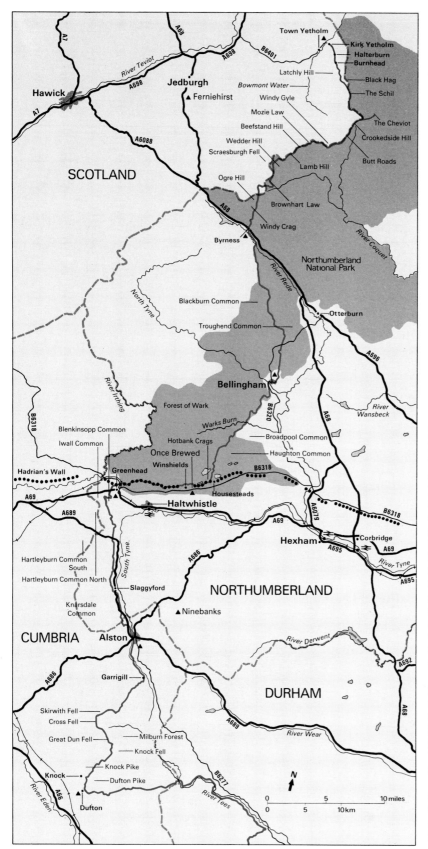

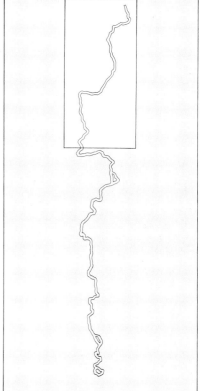

Middleton to Dufton
18 miles

The Path follows the river Tees north-west past the sparkling waters of Low Force and High Force, which have been disagreeably formalized and commercialized. There is a youth hostel a couple of miles further on at Langdon Beck. A short crag-hopping interlude brings you over the appropriately-named Falcon Clints and towards Cauldron Snout, once a thundering cascade in a superb wild setting, now somewhat tamed after the construction of the controversial Cow Green reservoir. This is still an impressive stretch, though, for all the car-parks, picnic areas and paved footpaths.

Now the walker is on what is arguably the loneliest and most majestic section of the whole Way. The route runs due west across desolate terrain alongside Maize Beck (wet feet are almost guaranteed) and at times seems endless. Then, so suddenly that you gasp, you are on the rim of High Cup Nick.

If I had to choose one spot that makes the entire walk worthwhile, it would be here. Unless it be high day or holiday, you will have the landscape to yourself: views of Skiddaw and

Coniston Old Man far off in the Lake District, Dufton Pike rising like an oversized burial mound in the middle distance, and at your feet a vast, scalloped glacial chasm with an almost sheer drop of 1000 feet to the bottom. It is a moment to savour, before you follow the Way as it winds round the very edge of the Whin Sill amphi-theatre and slowly descends into the Vale of Eden far below and the huddle of houses that marks the village of Dufton.

If you want a day off, Dufton, old, by-passed by the outside world and with a fine old pub without a bar, is a good place to choose. There is a shop and a post-office here, a splendidly wide, tree-lined main street and two camping-grounds.

Dufton to Alston
19 miles

The path now begins the long and at times arduous ascent and crossing of Knock Fell, Great Dun Fell and Cross Fell, at 2930 feet the highest peak along the Pennine Way. The views from this immense and lofty plateau are perhaps even more impressive than those from High Cup Nick. If the weather is clear, you will be able to see the distant Cheviots at the northern end of the Way. But there is a long way to go, and unless the weather is parti-cularly warm you will not want to linger, for even in high summer there can be a biting wind here.

There is a steepish descent now to join an old miners' track past Garrigill and on to Alston, an ancient and picturesque lead-mining centre. Alston is the highest market town in England (its altitude is 1000 feet) and the Pen-nine Way runs along the steep main street. There are good facilities here and a youth hostel on the outskirts.

Top right High Cup Nick, a 1000-foot natural chasm, perhaps the most dramatic spot along the entire path.

Centre right Hadrian's Wall, built from about AD 120 of large square stones piled some 14 feet high. In front of the Wall was a deep, wide ditch designed to slow attacking forces and expose them to fire from the Wall.

Right Part of Housesteads Fort, one of the major strongholds along the Wall. Here there were barracks, workshops, a temple, granaries and a headquarters building.

Alston to Housesteads
24 miles

A short distance north of Alston the path joins Maiden Way, a Roman road which it follows for some distance along the banks of the South Tyne before veering off and crossing Hartleyburn Common and Blenkinsopp Common to Greenhead. Here it meets Hadrian's Wall, which it winds along and alongside almost to Housesteads. This is the best-preserved fort along the ancient boundary, the major northern defensive line of the powerful Roman Empire, and there is a fine museum.

Between Greenhead and Housesteads there are a number of castles, small forts housing about fifty men, and other defensive features. The natural Whin Sill outcrop on top of which the wall runs between Winshields and Hotbank Crags is extremely impressive. The Once Brewed youth hostel east of Greenhead is a popular stopping place.

Housesteads to Bellingham
12 miles

Just west of Housesteads, the Pennine Way turns north once more and almost immediately dives into part of one of the largest afforested areas in western Europe. The Forest of Wark, one of six vast border plantations which blanket much of a landscape that quite recently was bare moorland, is exclusively coniferous and by and large only about seventy years old. Although the path is well marked, as indeed it must be, given the wealth of forest rides and firebreaks, a good map and compass are necessary. It is heavy going in places, especially in low-lying hollows, and the woods can be extremely dense and gloomy at times. Quite soon you break out of the dense forest, however, to cross Wark Burn and descend to the North Tyne valley and Bellingham.

Bellingham (pronounced Bellinjam) is a well-established market town, celebrated for its sheep sales, attended from far and wide. The town is unspoilt and full of fascinating nooks and crannies and has a charming square. There are pubs, a first-rate café and all the shops and banks a foot-traveller could want. There is also an information centre, a youth hostel and a camping-ground.

Bellingham to Byrness
17 miles

You leave the last staging-post along the Way (save for the miniscule hamlet of Byrness) on one of the ancient raiding routes (Bellingham itself was twice burned by invading Scotsmen), and the path passes close to the site of the battle of Otterburn of 1388. It is fine, open country at first as you climb out of the valley, and then there are more forestry plantations to be crossed through Redesdale before you reach Byrness on the A68. Here there is a youth hostel and a camping-ground close to Catcleugh reservoir.

Byrness to Kirk Yetholm
22 miles

Just north of Byrness, not far from Carter Bar, the Pennine Way crosses the Scottish border for the first time near Ogre Hill. Predictably the going is uphill and gruelling at times as you approach the Cheviots. At Windy Crag you are 1600 feet high and at Windy Gyle over 2000 feet. Make no mistake, this last stretch is as wild, remote and majestic as any tramped since the beginning of the Way. The culmination is the Cheviot summit plateau, 2675 feet high, before the path drops steeply at last to Kirk Yetholm.

At Kirk Yetholm, the older part of a twin settlement (the other, larger, part is Town Yetholm, on the eastern side of Bowmont Water), gipsy clans gathered for many years and successive nomadic kings were crowned. Cottages close by the Border Inn are still known as Gipsy Row, and one has the title of Gipsy Palace.

Opposite The Cheviot Hills at the northern end of the Way, where some lonely, tough going confronts the walker.

Top The main street of Alston, a pleasant, remote country town that was once the centre of a profitable lead-mining industry.

Above The welcome and celebrated pub on the green at Kirk Yetholm, northernmost point of the Pennine Way.

The West Highland Way

Officially opened 1980
Length: 95 miles
Going: hard

Ordnance Survey maps: 41, 50, 56, 57 and 64 (the official map, sold in a pack with the guidebook, covers the whole route in one sheet and is cheaper)

The West Highland Way, the first official long-distance footpath in Scotland, runs northwards from Milngavie, on the outskirts of Glasgow, to Fort William, in the heart of the West Highlands. It is a route of great character, passing through scenery of a scale and wild grandeur unmatched in England and Wales; and since the Way follows historic drove roads and military roads for much of its length, the walker enjoys a real sense of travel lacking on more artificial routes. The terrain becomes wilder as the Way goes north, from fertile farmland in Strath Blane and pleasant woodland along the shores of Loch Lomond, through wide mountain valleys in Glen Falloch, Strath Fillan and Glen Orchy to the vast wilderness of Rannoch Moor, culminating in a dramatic switchback over the rugged mountain ridges of Lochaber to the foot of Ben Nevis. This variety of landscape is matched by a wide range of interest in geology, wildlife and history.

Understandably, the West Highland Way is a more serious proposition than most of its counterparts south of the Border. Only short stretches, notably at the north end of Loch Lomond, give very rough walking; and the route is well marked–the Scottish waymark is a thistle within a hexagon. However, much of the northern half of the Way runs over remote high country where the average annual rainfall exceeds 100 inches and where gales are frequent. Walkers should therefore equip themselves for hill-walking and should be competent in map and compass work. May and June offer the best prospects for dry, clear, diamond-sharp weather.

While the Way often runs parallel and fairly close to road and railway, it passes through a good deal of virtually empty country where settlements with shops, accommodation and transport facilities are few and far between; a little advance planning is therefore advisable. Camping is the most flexible way to tackle the route–and, given good weather, much the most enjoyable.

Milngavie to Drymen
12 miles

The West Highland Way starts at Milngavie station, seven miles north of Glasgow city centre and readily accessible from there by 'bus or train. From Milngavie's busy shopping precinct the route passes quickly into open countryside, heading north beside the Allander Water into rural parkland and woodland. An old coach road gives easy walking by Craigallian Loch to the ridge crest at Carbeth, where in fine weather wide views northwards to Ben Lomond and the further Highland hills provide an early hint of this route's mountain grandeur.

Descending into the domestic farmland of Strath Blane, the Way follows an old railway line for 4 miles under the craggy scarp of the Campsie Fells, crosses the river Endrick at the quiet hamlet of Gartness and ambles along a country road to near Drymen, a pleasant village offering a fair range of shops and accommodation.

Drymen to Rowardennan
14 miles

Beyond Drymen the Way heads briefly east and then north-west on good forest tracks through the Garadhban Forest, with extensive views over Strath Endrick. A stretch over bracken-clad moorland and a stiff heathery climb lead to the superb viewpoint of Conic Hill, a steep hogsback ridge marking the Highland Boundary Fault. To the south is farmland, to the north mountain and moor.

A twisting descent now takes the walker south-westwards through a pinewood to the village of Balmaha on a bay of Loch Lomond, which here is wide, open and dotted with wooded islands. The Way winds along, partly by the Loch shore, occasionally on the rambling east shore road, but mainly in the fine mixed woods of the Queen Elizabeth Forest Park, to the hotel and youth hostel at Rowardennan below Ben Lomond.

Rowardennan to Inverarnan
14 miles

The next section of the Way, following the eastern shore of Loch Lomond to its head, is exhilaratingly rough. The Loch, now narrow and deep, is flanked by steep broken slopes clothed in oak and birchwood and rich in wildlife, including shy, shaggy, wild goats. This

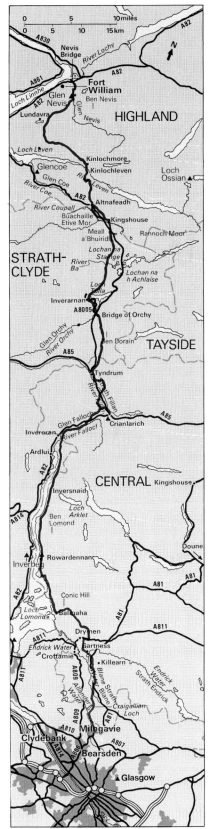

Loch Lomond, the largest stretch of inland water in Britain, whose eastern shore is followed by the West Highland Way.

area, Craigrostan, was a fitting haunt of the outlaw Rob Roy, immortalized by Sir Walter Scott. Parts of the route are trackless, while the stretch between the hotel at Inversnaid and the ruined farm at Doune is strenuous and calls for a little scrambling. North of Doune the Way rises to a saddle, giving contrasting views back down the loch and northwards to the high Tyndrum hills, before descending into lower Glen Falloch. Inverarnan has only a hotel, but Ardlui, two miles off-route, offers a hotel, camp-site and shop.

Inverarnan to Tyndrum
13 miles

In lower Glen Falloch the Way follows the river, which flows in a splendid series of falls, rapids and dark pools. Higher up, where the valley opens out and the woods give way to scattered pines, the route crosses the river to join the old military road, built in about 1750 to help to pacify the Highlands and now forming much of the northern part of the Way.

As the road crosses the low pass into Strath Fillan, providing magnificent views of the rugged Crianlarich hills, a spur from the Way descends to Crianlarich village. The main route continues through recent forestry plantations on the south side of the strath, then crosses to farmland on the north before climbing gently to Tyndrum – originally a lead-mining settlement and stance for cattle drovers, now a small tourist service centre.

Tyndrum to Kingshouse
19 miles

The pass leading into Glen Orchy is dominated by the great gully-seamed peak of Ben Dorain, signifying that the Way is now truly in mountain country. The route runs parallel to the railway under Dorain's western slope, crosses the Orchy at the tiny settlement of Bridge of Orchy and takes the hill road over Mam Carraigh to the little hotel at Inveroran. Rounding Loch Tulla, it climbs steadily on to Rannoch Moor, the remotest and wildest section of the Way. On the left the high ridges of the Blackmount enclose the deep-cut Coire Ba, haunt of red deer; to the right, the moor stretches away in a desolation of peat-bog, boulders, hummocks and lochans. As it rounds the flank of Meall a'Bhuiridh, the Way descends gradually towards Glen Coe. The historic hotel of Kingshouse lies in a moorland bowl amidst some of the noblest mountain scenery in Britain.

Kingshouse to Kinlochleven
9 miles

Two alternatives are available as the Way runs west into the portals of Glen Coe: the old road under Beinn a'Chrulaiste, giving wide views, or a trackless route by the river, close under the gaunt crags of Buachaille Etive Mor. At Altnafeadh the military road strikes uphill on the zig-zags of the Devil's Staircase, giving a fairly easy ascent to the highest point on the Way (1800 feet) and a magnificent mountain prospect northwards.

From the pass the path swings downhill round rugged spurs before plunging into the valley bottom at Kinlochleven, an unattractive and incongruous factory town where aluminium is smelted by hydro-electricity generated from the Blackwater reservoir on Rannoch Moor. Here you can find accommodation and the widest range of shops since Drymen.

Kinlochleven to Fort William
14 miles

From sea-level at Kinlochleven the Way climbs steeply, with spectacular views across to the Glen Coe hills, into the Lairigmor pass under the rocky flanks of the Mamores. The pass is enclosed and rather bleak until the route turns northwards to the woodland and little loch at Lundavra. Here the Way deserts the military road and contours through plantations, the massive bulk of Ben Nevis looming ahead, to attain a col above Glen Nevis, close by the Iron Age fort of Dun Deardail. A short, steep descent leads to a forest track, which sidles gently into the glen to join the public road down to Nevis Bridge. There, less than a mile from the urban facilities of Fort William, the West Highland Way ends. For those with time and energy to spare, the ascent of Ben Nevis offers a satisfying finale.

The Best of British Walks

Despite the real thrill of walking the long-distance footpaths of Britain, there are many occasions on which limited time and resources will not permit such expeditions. In these cases, some of the many other splendid walking areas throughout the country may provide the answer. At any rate, every walk away from cars and concrete will be its own reward.

The following short chapters cover some of my own favourite areas, some, such as the National Parks, well known, others more secret and therefore less crowded. Some are as tough as the toughest of the long-distance paths, while others provide easier going. So, whether for three hours or three weeks, and whatever your capability, I hope you will share my pleasure in two-legged locomotion.

The view towards Dartmeet from Combestone Tor on the southern edge of the Dartmoor National Park. Britain's National Parks are a haven for walkers and naturalists alike–indeed for all country-lovers–and contain some of the most scenic, and on occasions the most challenging, footpaths the country has to offer.

A personal selection of some of the country's best paths

Dartmoor National Park
Exmoor National Park and the
 Quantocks
The New Forest
The Isle of Wight
East Kent
East Anglia
The Oxfordshire Way
The Cotswolds
The Wye Valley
The Malvern Hills
The Brecon Beacons
 National Park and
the Cambrian Mountains
Snowdonia National Park
The Shropshire Hills
The Peak District National Park
The Viking Way
The Yorkshire Dales
 National Park
The North York Moors
 National Park
The Forest of Bowland
The Lake District National Park
Northumberland National Park
Scotland

Dartmoor National Park

The 365 square miles of the Dartmoor National Park are one of the last untamed stretches of country in southern England. The moor is a place of contrasts. Within a few miles of massive granite tors and bleak wind-swept uplands are lush and beautiful river valleys. Friendly and seductive in the sunshine, the land is stern, even eerie when the swirling mists descend. Despite some treacherous bogs, how-ever, the only real danger to the walker is from the army ranges around Cut Hill; only the foolhardy will ignore the red flags and warning signs. None the less, there are many areas devoid of recognized tracks and paths, and a walk on Dartmoor should not be undertaken casually.

The Dartmoor the tourist sees con-sists of the areas along the main roads and all the scenic high spots a car or coach can reach. Two Bridges is the recognized centre for these visitors. The rest of the moor belongs to the enthusiastic walker.

The routes along footpaths and back lanes from Widecombe in the Moor to Haytor Rocks and along the ancient Abbots Way from Buckfastleigh (near Buckfast Abbey) to Princetown are splendid examples of all that Dartmoor has to offer. There are rushing water-courses, picturesque clapper bridges, huddled hamlets and a host of Bronze Age remains. And for company you will have a variety of wildlife and free-ranging cattle, sheep and ponies.

Postbridge, near the centre of the moor, is a good walking centre, with paths in many directions, including some to Cut Hill. Although Dartmeet, between Two Bridges and Ashburton, is very popular with motorists, a short walk along the river path will bring seclusion and delightful scenery.

Among the best walks on Dartmoor are those around Chagford. From this charming village you can follow the Teign valley east to Steps Bridge via the impressive pack-horse Fingle Bridge or take the ancient Mariners Way between the hamlet of Throwleigh and Widecombe. The Way—most of which is now long since lost—ran across the Peninsula from Bideford to Dartmouth and is said to have been used by sailors. Both these routes offer 10 miles or more of continuous waymarked path

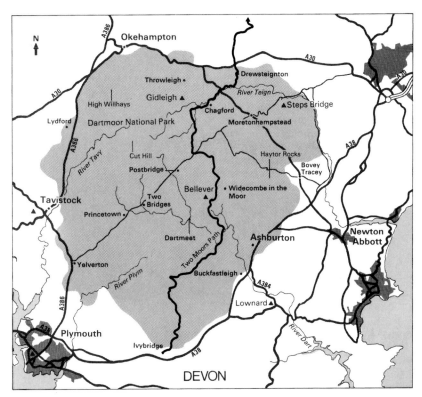

amid scenery that is as enchanting as any in the West Country.

The loftiest spot in the Park is High Willhays (2038 feet), a magnificent viewpoint not far south of Okehamp-ton. There is an excellent choice of accommodation and camping-grounds near here, along the busy A30. Tavis-

Saddle Tor near Widecombe in the Moor, an excellent centre for exploring a wide variety of Dartmoor footpaths.

tock, in the south-west corner of the Park, is an alternative base, and the lovely Tavy valley north-west of the town is outstandingly beautiful.

Exmoor National Park and the Quantocks

The Two Moors Way, opened in 1976, provides a pleasant link between Dartmoor and Exmoor. It runs for 103 miles right across Devon along existing paths and country roads between Ivybridge in the south and Lynmouth in the north. The going can often be wet and muddy, and the Way is hilly and by no means always easy walking. The terrain includes open, high moorland as well as river valleys and green lanes.

Exmoor National Park—the smallest in Britain—offers spectacular scenery of two kinds, coastal and wooded. Walkers on the South-West Peninsula Coast Path can enjoy the former, while inland there is a grand variety of historic and natural beauty amid a landscape that might almost have been created with the walker in mind.

The best walking routes are along the steep and richly wooded combes of the water-courses that meander from the heather-clad plateaux to form the rivers Exe, Barle, Mole and the East and West Lyn. The West Lyn's steep, sharp descent from the high moor was partly responsible for the tragic Lynmouth flood disaster in 1952. Most of Exmoor's rivers are somewhat gentler of character, however, especially those that flow south of Dunkery Beacon, at 1705 feet the highest point in the Park.

The Beacon's command of the central heights makes it an obvious target for walkers. The waymarked route from isolated Wheddon Cross on the A396 between Dunster and Dulverton offers a windswept trudge with wide horizons. Another dramatic path leads from Luccombe, coastwards of the great rounded hill.

My own favourite Exmoor walk is the intriguing path from Withypool to Tarr Steps, one of the most impressive clapper bridges in England. This memorable 4-mile route runs almost entirely alongside the banks of the sparkling Barle through a secluded part of the National Park where you may be lucky enough to spot red deer or even otters. The landscape in autumn is a feast for the eye, a riot of glossy green and burnished gold.

Lorna Doone enthusiasts will want to visit Oare village where, in the little fourteenth-century church, Lorna was shot by Carver Doone on her wedding day. Not far away at Malsmead is

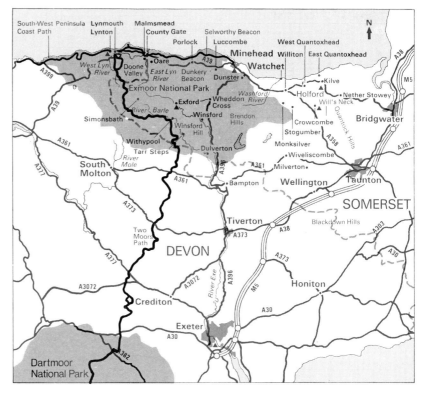

The seventeenth-century Yarn Market at Dunster and, behind it, the castle. The village, on the edge of Exmoor and near the coast, is an excellent walking centre.

Lorna Doone Farm. There is a pretty and evocative 5-mile circular walk from Oare, just off the A39 near County Gate, via the farm and thence to the Blackmore Memorial and the delightful Badgworthy Water.

At the eastern end of Exmoor the Brendon Hills slope gently down to the vale country of Williton, Monksilver and Stogumber, then rise again as the Quantocks. These are just under 40 square miles of rounded green hills, combes and bracken-carpeted slopes, culminating in the splendid West Quantoxhead and Wills Neck, southeast of Crowcombe. Wills Neck is the highest point of the hill line (1260 feet above sea level), which is never broader than about 4 miles. The whole 12-mile ridge is an easy walk.

Crowcombe is a good centre for shorter walks. The Quantock Forest Trail is located midway between here Bridge. And, from the picture-postcard hamlet of East Quantoxhead, and Nether Stowey, at Seven Wells there is a superb circular hill route inland and another coastwards to the cliffs and the ruins of Kilve Priory.

The New Forest

The Pride of Hampshire, that magnificent 20-mile stretch of woodland and heath between Southampton and Bournemouth, is ideal territory for the walker and camper. There is a first-class network of camping-grounds, some of which make special provision for lightweight campers and hikers. There is a seasonal information office in Lyndhurst, the main forest town, where a list of camp sites is obtainable, together with maps and guides of the best walking areas.

There are some interesting short waymarked walks around Rhinefield, including the Boulderwood Walk and the Tall Trees walk. Not far north is the famous Rufus Stone where, it is said, William Rufus was accidentally killed when Sir Walter Tyrell loosed a careless arrow. And just to the south, in the graveyard of Minstead church, lies another famous Englishman, Sir Arthur Conan Doyle.

A splendid day-long walk begins from Minstead south-west through wooded enclosures and across open

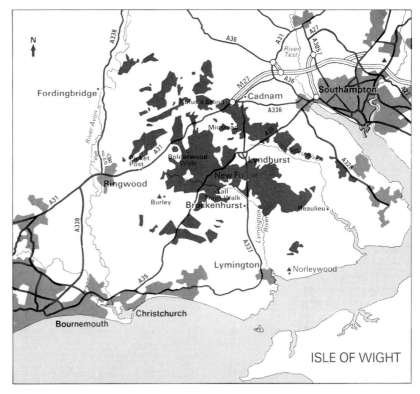

heath to Picket Post, then on to Burley and the camping-ground at Holmsley. Of course you can also plot your own route around the Forest, seeking the least-used tracks and minor roads during the day and using the Forestry Commission camping-grounds overnight.

The New Forest is an excellent training-ground for walkers, for the terrain, though undulating, is not too

severe. The well-wooded sections do require a fair amount of map and compass work, however, even though villages and hamlets are nearly always nearby. Yet along the less-frequented forest rides, the walker has the distinct feeling of being amid genuinely untamed country, and roe deer and wild ponies may be the only company, even in high summer.

Typical walking country in the New Forest. Established by William the Conqueror as a royal hunting preserve and jealously guarded by generations of his successors, the Forest is now one of the largest areas of open country in the south of England, a pleasant mixture of wood and heathland crossed by innumerable paths.

The Isle of Wight

The Isle of Wight is best visited in winter. The days may be shorter then, but the climate remains remarkably balmy, and the islanders, hard pressed during the summer, are altogether more relaxed and friendly.

The chalk downs of this green and pleasant island are a walker's paradise. There is an excellent network of routes, including a 60-mile coastal path, and no less than seven long-distance trails.

West Wight is perhaps the best walking area of all. The least-crowded part of the island, it offers splendid views and invigorating going. The downs that provide such pleasant walking extend the length of the island, from The Needles to Culver Cliff, Bembridge. The ridge is the remains of a forward edge of two gigantic billows raised in the earth's crust at the time the continental alps were being formed, some 20 million years ago.

The Tennyson Trail

The Tennyson Trail runs through the heart of West Wight. The trail is named after Lord Tennyson, who in 1927 presented some 150 acres of the downland near the Tennyson Monument to the National Trust in memory of his father, the Poet Laureate. It was he who declared that the air on the downs was worth sixpence a pint.

The 15-mile route starts about a mile from Newport, near Carisbrooke Castle, built on the remains of a Roman fort and famous later as the prison that held Charles I. A gentle ascent takes the walker across Brightstone Down and then along the fringe of Brightstone Forest, a Forestry Commission plantation. Although not the highest point in the island, Brightstone Down is a fine vantage point from which the whole length of the island can be caught in one breathtaking sweep.

The path, which here coincides briefly with the Jubilee Trail, climbs again to a summit burial mound, the Long Stone, dating from about 3000 BC. There are more fine views of the chalk cliffs on the descent to Freshwater Bay, and the path rises again to Tennyson Down and The Needles, the remains of the great chalk barrier that once joined the island to the mainland. It is advisable to keep clear of cliff edges around here. From the splendid headland, the path winds

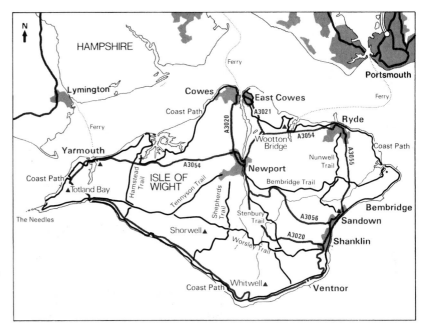

down to Alum Bay, famous for its coloured sands. Up to twelve may be counted, and the best time to see them is after rain. The final stretch of the Trail has been designated a bird sanctuary, and guillemots, razorbills, kittiwakes and puffins may be seen.

Rolling downland at Culver Cliff on the eastern edge of the Isle of Wight. The extensive network of waymarked trails running over the entire island provides enjoyable walking through magnificent country and coastal landscapes.

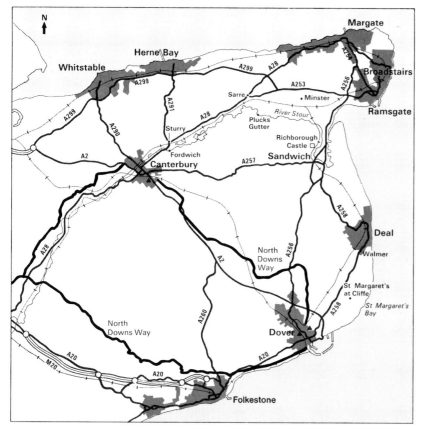

East Kent

The fine triangle of coast and orchard country between Dover, Sandwich and Canterbury is well worth exploring on foot. One side of the triangle is defined by the northern loop of the North Downs Way which runs from Canterbury over Barham Downs and above Folkestone to Dover.

Although the official Way stops in Dover, the cliff-top path continues from the mighty castle and ascends the chalk cliffs high above the bustling port and the cross-Channel ferry terminals. On really clear days mainland Europe seems tantalisingly near as you walk across the dramatic white cliffs, perhaps the most evocative of all the symbols of England. War-time debris is a reminder that this area–'Hellfire Corner' as it was nicknamed–suffered much from air attack and long-range guns. Passing Martello towers, lighthouses and coastguard lookouts in quick succession, the Path finishes in the Churchill Memorial Park above charming St Margaret's Bay, its superb seascapes making a most fitting setting for the national hero.

Having descended from the cliffs, the walker passes Walmer castle, built by Henry VIII as part of his system of coastal defences and now the official residence of the Lord Warden of the Cinque Ports. Beyond Deal, the Path follows the foreshore along sand dunes and golf courses and then turns inland to Sandwich.

Sandwich was for many centuries a busy port, as its picturesque and ancient buildings testify. Canute landed here in 1013, as did pilgrims bound for Canterbury, merchants and other travellers. Today the sea has receded and the estuary has silted up. Richborough Castle, one and a half miles north of the town, is an awesome Roman stronghold and site of the Roman landing in AD43.

From Sandwich the walker can make his way along farm lanes and footpaths, roughly tracing the river Stour, to the quaintly-named Plucks Gutter and thence on through an unknown medieval Kent where time really does stand still to Sturry and Fordwich. Fordwich, the port for Canterbury in the Middle Ages, boasts a tiny fifteenth-century town hall in a superb state of preservation and an ancient church. From here it is only a short distance to Canterbury.

St Margaret's Bay, the usual English landfall for cross-Channel swimmers and a pleasant rest spot on the coastal path between Dover and Deal.

East Anglia

Many people would hardly consider East Anglia to be good walking country. Flat terrain, fenland in the north-east of the region and Broads in the west, and perhaps the most intensively farmed land in the whole country, would appear to combine to prevent the walker getting into his stride.

Although this is to some extent true, it is not entirely the case, and those prepared to explore a little will find some pleasant walking country. To be sure, there are no regal heights, but Norfolk does have some gentle hill-country along a short coastal strip in the north of the county; in Suffolk there are some outstanding nature reserves best seen–indeed often only accessible–on foot. What the whole of East Anglia can claim is a benign climate with a great deal of sun and, as a consequence, a vast population of wild life. The area is a bird-watcher's delight, and there is always a rich variety of flora and fauna to study.

Thetford Chase in the Suffolk/Norfolk border country is a marvellous swathe of forest and heathland. At its heart is Santon Downham, some five miles from Thetford, prettily set down beside the narrow river Ouse. Although this forest now seems so great, it is comparatively young, for tree-planting only began after the First World War. There were fears that the whole of the Brecklands would be suffocated under conifers. In fact the scheme has been highly successful, and the original sandy, almost tree-less terrain has changed beyond recognition, replaced by a pleasant mixture of alternating heath and woodland. There is a forestry camping-ground and a number of intriguing waymarked paths, one of which leads to the fascinating Neolithic flint mines at Grime's Graves, which are open to visitors.

The beautiful low cliffs of the Suffolk coast are still wild and remote, mainly the haunt of seabirds and intrepid foreshore walkers. There are interesting bird sanctuaries at Dunwich (Minsmere), Thorpeness and Orford Ness, an immense shingle spit, the largest along the east coast.

Much of the north Norfolk coast is very different from the rest of East Anglia's shores. Here there are hills, and impressive they are too, especially around Upper Sheringham and rolling

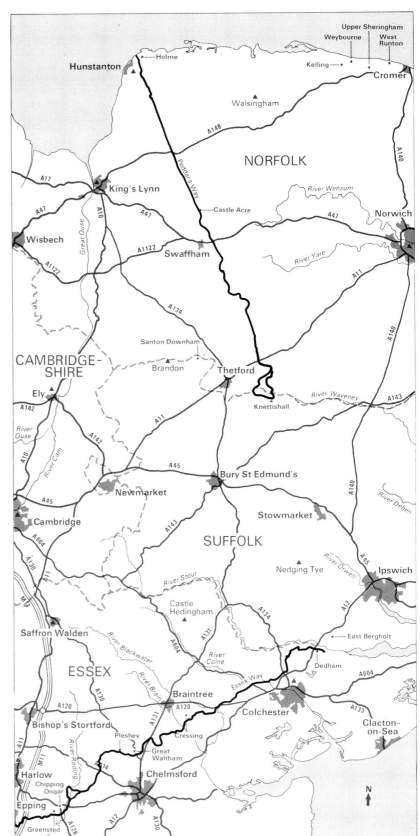

St Andrew's Church at Greensted, Essex, thought to have been built early in the eleventh century to receive the body of St Edmund the martyr on its journey from London to Bury St Edmunds. Oak tree trunks were used for the exterior walls, the rounded sides being positioned to the outside.

Kelling Heath, inland from Weybourne. A popular walking area is near Roman Camp in a lofty wooded setting a couple of miles inland from West Runton.

There are two lengthy waymarked routes in East Anglia. One, the Essex Way, in the very south of the region, runs through a pleasant, little-known area of the Essex countryside. The other, Peddars Way, is an ancient track connecting two walking areas already mentioned, the north Norfolk coast and the Brecklands near Thetford.

The Essex Way

This route offers easy footpath and country lane walking for 50 miles across the Essex hinterland. It is gently undulating, open landscape in the main, though some woodland and coppices are encountered. It is surprisingly rural once Epping, the starting-point, has been left behind.

There is some fascinating history along the Way. Greensted boasts what may be the oldest wooden church in the world–it was built in Saxon times–and at Pleshey there is a majestic Norman castle; the village still huddles inside the outer rampart and ditch. At

Cressing there are two remarkable feed-barns (one weather-boarded, the other brick-nogged), the only remains of the Knights Templar, who settled here in 1135. The Way ends at Dedham where Constable went to school. About a mile away, just across the Suffolk border, is Flatford Mill, made famous by him.

The kind terrain makes brisk walking at a steady pace possible. There is a camping-ground at East Bergholt at the eastern end of the Way, which is open all year.

Peddars Way

Peddars Way was almost certainly built by the Roman occupying forces in the years after they had defeated the uprising led by Queen Boadicea in AD 60. Like all Roman roads, it was driven straight across country, taking little or no account of obstacles in its path. Its purpose is uncertain. It certainly enabled the Romans to exercise greater control of the districts through which it ran. It also linked London and Essex, areas already firmly controlled by the Romans, with the Wash and thus with Lincolnshire as well, for there may well have been a ferry across the Wash.

After the Roman withdrawal the Way was no doubt used by successive invaders from Scandinavia and, in the Middle Ages, by travellers of all kinds, itinerant pedlars, drovers and pilgrims. Its importance gradually declined, at least partly because it did not connect any major settlements, until it fell into complete disuse when the railways brought a faster and effortless means of travelling.

The route today runs for about 50 miles between Knettishall on the Suffolk/Norfolk border and Holme on the Wash. About 30 miles of the original Way are followed; for the other 20 a nearby alternative is way-marked to avoid substantial stretches on metalled roads. The going is easy through a pleasant landscape. Heavy undergrowth may occasionally obstruct the path, which also runs across the Stanford Battle Area, still used by the army. You must keep strictly to the waymarked route here.

There are plans to establish an official long-distance path in East Anglia. The first half will probably run along the present route of Peddars Way, to be followed by a coastal section from Hunstanton to Cromer.

The Oxfordshire Way

The Oxfordshire Way provides a walkers' link between two areas of outstandingly beautiful areas, the Cotswolds and the Chilterns. Some 65 miles long, it runs between Bourton-on-the-Water in Gloucestershire and Henley-on-Thames in Oxfordshire. The section between Bledington and Stonefield, some 12½ miles, is a bridleway, and there are many other shorter stretches on which horse-riders are also permitted.

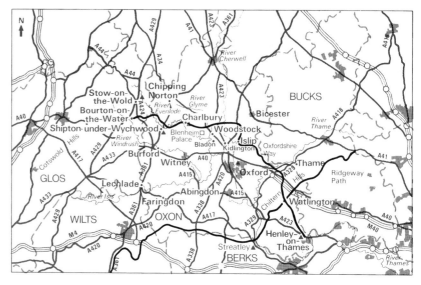

The words of the Council for the Preservation of Rural England, whose Oxfordshire branch was responsible for creating the route, best describe the Way. It runs 'along the ancient tracks of the county, through meadows and woods, along quiet river valleys and over windy escarpments, by many a delightful village'. It passes, too, a number of charming rivers, the Windrush, the Evenlode, the Cherwell and the Thame, and meets the Thames at Henley, home of the famous regatta held every year in July.

This part of England will also appeal to walkers with a sense of history. At Woodstock, a short way south of the path, lies Blenheim Palace, given to the Duke of Marlborough by the nation in gratitude for his success in the wars against France. Winston Churchill was born here and buried in the churchyard at Bladon just to the south; a modest headstone marks his grave. Not far from Thame is the fifteenth-century Ryecote Chapel with an attractive barrel roof and carved benches.

There is an excellent riverside camping-ground called Cassington Mill near Kidlington which makes a good midway base and three youth hostels for those who prefer a more solid roof over their heads at night. The Way is easy walking over the entire route, though there may be one or two muddy sections in winter.

Bourton-on-the-Water, a charming village of Cotswold-stone houses at the western end of the Oxfordshire Way.

The Cotswolds

During the Middle Ages, the Cotswold hills, which provided countless square miles of grazing, were one of the great wool-trading areas of Britain. Local communities grew rich and stable, building solid golden-stone houses and churches. This is English agricultural landscape at its prettiest and most permanent, and there are still many miles of tracks and footways along which drovers once guided their flocks.

Broadway–sometimes called the Gateway to the Cotswolds–is a good base for short walks and also offers a near-perfect example of how to use Cotswold stone to its best: a most handsome, if heavily visited, town. Other Cotswold delights are Stow-on-the-Wold, Castle Combe, Stanton, Birdlip and Bilbury.

In between the villages there is excellent walking, almost always across a fine open landscape of rolling uplands. Coopers Hill, near Painswick, is the setting for the celebrated Cheese-Rolling contest each spring, and Cleeve Cloud Hill, 1083 feet, is the highest in the Cotswold range.

The Cotswold Way is a delightful–and extremely popular–path running along almost the entire length of the Cotswold escarpment from Chipping

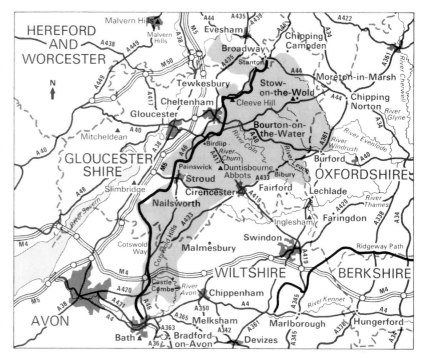

Campden to Bath. It passes near many historic sites and–an important feature for the walker–near numerous towns and villages where overnight accommodation may be obtained. The path itself constantly delights the eye, and the peaceful landscape of rolling hills and fine, wide views as far as the Black Mountains and the Malvern and Shropshire Hills provides a sense of repose.

The view towards Tewkesbury from Belas Knap, a Stone Age long barrow set high in the Cotswold hills between Winchcombe and Twickenham.

The Wye Valley

The slow and tortuous descent towards the sea of the river Wye from its source in the Cambrian mountains creates some magnificent scenery and excellent riverside walking. Offa's Dyke Path runs through the lower Wye valley, near Tintern Abbey. In the upper valley, along the western fringes of the ancient Forest of Dean, there is more majestic walking.

The Forest (once widely worked for coal and other mineral wealth) is now largely administered by the Forestry Commission, which provides a strategic, spacious camping-ground near Coleford, Gloucestershire. There are a number of waymarked walks direct from the site, one of which leads to the limestone precipices of the Wye Gorge at Symonds Yat. Every corner of the forest is open to visitors, and there is much to see, from relics of prehistoric life at King Arthur's Cave in Lord's Wood at Welshbury to an abundance of wild-life. Sheep, cattle, pigs, geese and even chickens range freely over unfenced grazing, a rare sight in today's countryside.

The Wye Valley Walk

Much further upstream, the Wye Valley Walk is a 36-mile route from Hay-on-Wye to Rhayader.

The path from snug Hay follows the river faithfully at first and touches it periodically at Glasbury, Erwood, Builth, Newbridge, Rhayader and a number of hamlets in between. The scenery is varied and magnificent all the way, with some fine views of the Black Mountain foothills and the wooded river valley. Between Hay and Erwood (12½ miles), you pass Maesyronen Chapel, said to be the oldest place of worship in Wales, and also Llangoed Castle–which you can see but may not enter–designed by Clough William-Ellis, the architect of the Italianate Port Meirion.

Between Erwood and Builth there is the inn where Henry Mayhew, fleeing from creditors, had the idea of founding *Punch,* the fantastic profusion of Aberedw Rocks and Llewelyn's Cave, where the prince is said to have hidden from the pursuing English. Builth Wells, a famous spa since Roman times, is followed by Penddol Rocks and Rapids *en route* to Newbridge and a path that climbs easily to some 1000 feet, giving splendid

views over surprisingly wild country. After Newbridge there is some farm-lane walking and then heady vistas over the Elan valley and the Wye before the path drops down to Rhayader, a picturesque market town on the fringe of some of the wildest country in Wales.

The River Wye seen from Symonds Yat, one of the most magnificent sections on what can claim to be among the country's finest rivers. There is good walking along and near the river valley from its Welsh source until it meets the estuary of the Severn just below Chepstow.

The Malvern Hills

It is the abruptness with which the slim and compact Malverns rise up out of the low-lying plain that makes them so intriguing and so noticeable from far off. Known affectionately as Elgar's hills after the composer, who lived for many years nearby and often walked them, the Malverns are a mere 10 miles or so long and hardly more than a few hundred yards wide for much of this distance. Nevetheless, every mile is full of interest, and given good weather conditions the views are breathtaking.

Although surrounded by busy roads and settlements and walked and ridden by tens of thousands, the Malverns manage to retain a sense of magic, hard to define but tangible enough for those who have already enjoyed them. The atmosphere, especially early on a spring morning, can be exhilarating, and for variety and excitement in a day's walk the range can hardly be rivalled. Those not used to hill-walking may find the ridge surprisingly severe; Malvern Wells is a good base for shorter expeditions.

Although the hills extend a little further to the north, the logical starting-point for most walkers is Malvern itself, a delightful spa town nestling just below the northern end of the scarp. Around the shoulder of North Hill stupendous views across the upper Severn valley begin to unfold. Clear way-marking takes the walker on to Worcester Beacon, at 1394 feet king of the Malvern peaks, then over a wonderful switch-back ridge with views to both east and west. A swooping descent to Wyche Cutting follows and then a surprisingly stiff and prolonged climb to the Herefordshire Beacon, a huge Iron Age hill fort. The Path winds on above Malvern reservoir and past Giant's Cave and Red Earl's Dyke. Eastnor Park and its tall obelisk mark the south-western fringe of the range, along which the A438 runs between Hereford and Tewkesbury, although there are two hills, Ragged Stone and Cheese End, further south.

Herefordshire Beacon, an unmistakeable landmark 1174 feet high on the ridge of the Malvern Hills. The Iron Age hill fort here, known as British Camp, encompassed no less than 32 acres; the mound on top is a later addition, however, dating from the eleventh or twelfth centuries.

The Brecon Beacons National Park and the Cambrian Mountains

The Brecon Beacons National Park holds over 500 square miles of slumbering round-tops and fertile river valleys, occasionally broken by massive, even awe-inspiring scarps. The Park includes the Black Mountains, through which Offa's Dyke Path runs, an area that offers excellent walking prospects, as do the stern Brecon Beacons themselves, nearly 3000 feet high.

Llangorse Lake in the slightly gentler country of the wide, green Usk valley is an attractive base with a number of camping-grounds, the nearby wooded foothills enticing the walker to explore. There are some superb hill-paths in almost every direction; the valley between Crickhowell and Brecon town is particularly fruitful.

One classic high-level path starts some 9 miles south-west of Brecon alongside the A470, ascending from the Storey Arms to Pen y Fan summit, at 2906 feet the highest in the range. The route is well marked but hard going in places and should not be attempted in foul weather. When the sun is shining, however, and the wind light, the walk will elevate the spirits as much as the body. The views from the summit ridge are memorable.

In total contrast is the Monmouth & Brecon Canal, which winds for over 30 miles from Brecon to the south-east corner of the National Park just above Pontypool. Many visitors walk the whole length of the towpath.

North-west of the Brecons, between Rhayader and Aberystwyth, are the Cambrian Mountains. Though not quite so spectacular as the famous peaks of Snowdonia just to the north, they are impressive enough, especially the Plynlimon group. The highest of these—Plynlimon Fawr—rises to 2468 feet high above Nant-y-moch reservoir. There is a fine and fairly easy ascent of this giant from alongside the A44 some 5 miles north-east of Devil's Bridge, at Eisteddfa-Gurig Farm. A well-marked miners' track takes walkers past some old lead workings to the summit and rewards them with some splendid panoramas right across Wales and beyond to Shropshire. The climb should only be attempted in good weather, however.

There is particularly pleasant walking along the Elan river past the Garreg Ddu, Craig Goch and Penygarreg reservoirs, which are far more attractive than one might think. Devil's Bridge, a dozen miles inland from Aberystwyth, has long been a popular beauty spot. But not far from the famous trio of bridges over the Mynach Falls you can find seclusion on the grand scale: simply follow the river Rheidol and then take the path above Rheidol Gorge.

Llangorse Lake and the distant Brecon Beacons. The National Park is a walker's paradise, with routes across windswept hilltops and through gentle low country.

Snowdonia National Park

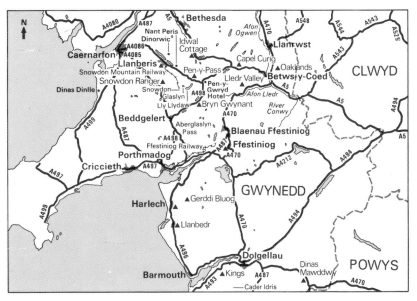

Y-Wyddfa, the highest mountain in all England and Wales, thrusts its summit no less than 3560 feet above sea level, surrounded by a host of only slightly less majestic neighbours. Better known, of course, as Mount Snowdon, this mighty centrepiece of the National Park is one of many wild mountains of emerald green below stern grey peaks, softened by a scattering of lakes, forests and richly-wooded valleys.

It scarcely matters along which approach road you come, for they are all exceptionally beautiful: through the Dovey valley and around Cader Idris to Dolgellau; the central route via Lake Bala to Blaenau Ffestiniog; or through Betws-y-Coed, under the shadow of Snowdon itself, and on through Llanberis Pass. Besides the magnificent mountain scenery, the area offers a series of majestic castles built by Edward I to subdue the Welsh and a fine coastline along the bays of Cardigan, Caernarfon and Conwy. The wide sandy beaches below Caernarfon at Dinas Dinlle, at Pwllheli on the Llyn Peninsula and between Barmouth and Harlech Castle are safe, spacious and, when the sun shines, superb.

The sun does not shine all the time in Snowdonia, though, and for walkers quality rainwear is obligatory, together with woollies and duvets, for even in summer it can be decidedly fresh when dusk falls. However, one of the virtues of this area is that the mountains act as a cloud magnet. Thus if fair weather is a priority, make your base in the foothills rather than in the mountains.

The most direct route into the central massif is the steadily ascending A4085 from Caernarfon to Beddgelert Forest. In a superb setting just a mile short of Beddgelert village there is a Forestry Commission camping-ground, one of the most popular in all Wales. Snowdon is but a short distance away, and there is a choice of way-marked walks and forest trails, plus fishing and pony-trekking. Two of the most enjoyable paths around here ascend Moel Hebog (some rock-scrambling is involved) and lead down the majestic Aberglaslyn Pass from Beddgelert.

The road from Beddgelert to Llanberis is also a spectacular route. It passes the Pen-y-Gwryd Hotel, the training quarters of the team that climbed Everest in 1953, and the Pen-y-Pass youth hostel. Two paths to the summit of Snowdon start here, the Miners' Track and the Pyg Track. This extremely popular circular route offers almost 8 miles of summit walking. The views across Llyn Llydaw and Glaslyn from the horseshoe path are unforgettable. Around Nant Peris, climbers can usually be spotted high above, clinging like flies to the sheer walls. You can join them on the tops if you feel so inclined, using the well-trodden hill path from Nant Peris across to the A5, some 5 miles away. In between the reward is Snowdonia at its most dramatic.

The huge new power-station just above Llanberis, itself almost dwarfed by the even larger excavations at the Dinorwic slate mines, is almost complete. Landscaping should ensure that it will scarcely intrude into this most beautiful pass.

On the eastern side of the Park, Betws-y-Coed is a magnet for those who enjoy walks in wooded river valleys. Swallow Falls is a high spot, but inevitably it is somewhat over-visited, and indeed Betws itself caters rather too much for tourists.

There are splendid views on the road south from Betws, which at first follows the steep wooded valley of the river Lledr and then climbs to cross wild open moors. It then descends to Blaenau Ffestiniog, where there is an information centre and conducted tours of the famous slate mine.

The stern, grey-blue peaks and glittering lakes of Snowdonia make a magnificent visual reward for the adventurous.

South again from here lies Cader Idris, a mighty peak 2927 feet high. There are footpaths to the summit from both Dolgellau and Towyn. Although the route from Towyn is easier, neither should be tackled by novices if the weather is at all doubtful; this country is very much the province of the experienced hill-walker.

The Shropshire Hills

A little more than halfway between Birmingham and the Welsh border, the Shropshire hills offer the walker the pleasing prospect of quiet seclusion amid green hills. Here four distinct ridges await exploration. Running roughly south-east to north-west they are: the Clee Hills, between Ludlow and Bridgnorth; Wenlock Edge, between Craven Arms and Much Wenlock; the unmistakeable Long Mynd west of Church Stretton; and, finally, the Stiperstones, north of Bishop's Castle. In addition the Wrekin stands aside on its own some way to the north-east, divided from the main group by the Severn valley.

Beloved by every Salopian and immortalized in A. E. Housman's *Shropshire Lad,* The Wrekin stands proudly above the surrounding low-land. Although it is not the highest of the Shropshire hills—at 1790 feet Brown Clee wins this honour—it is certainly very distinctive, particularly when viewed from south of the Severn.

Much Wenlock is an excellent starting-point for the 16 miles of hill walks and fine views on Wenlock Edge. Alternatively you might try either of the two minor roads that flank the rising scarp at the northern end.

The extraordinary shape of the Long Mynd dominates the skyline for miles around. One of the best stretches can be reached from the Cardingmill Valley Road from Church Stretton. The hill path climbs westwards for a couple of miles to the 1695-foot summit. The panoramas from the rounded top are marvellous, particularly of the serrated Stiperstones.

The Stiperstones are even more impressive close up than from a distance. These splintered limestone crags, 1700 feet high, are as rugged as any in central England. An inviting footpath runs along the summit ridge for two or three miles.

There is plentiful and varied accommodation at Church Stretton and Much Wenlock, camping-grounds at Craven Arms and Ludlow and a farm site at Ratlinghope in the shadow of the Long Mynd.

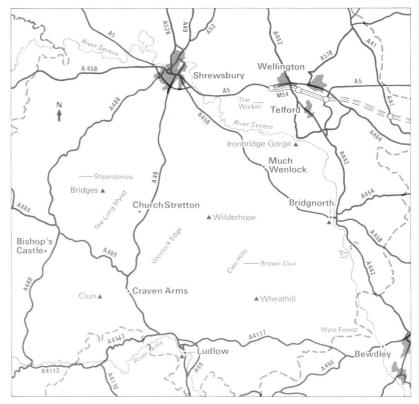

The view from Wenlock Edge, one of the four eminently walkable ridges of the Shropshire Hills. This is classic English countryside at its very best.

The Peak District National Park

The Peak District is so rich that, no matter how many times you visit it, you are always rewarded by some new and interesting aspect. To begin with, there are two distinctly different areas within the National Park. The Dark Peak is the stern and rugged high country lying roughly north of a line drawn between Chapel-en-le-Frith and Castleton and dominated by the brooding presence of Kinder Scout, Bleaklow and Black Hill. It is through these wild peat moors that the Pennine Way, Britain's most romantic long-distance path, winds.

South of the line is the gentler White Peak, so called after the grey-white limestone outcrops amid the emerald-green countryside. This rugged plateau country is criss-crossed by friendly wooded valleys fed by the rivers Derwent, Dove, Wye and Manifold.

Castleton, approximately at the centre of 500 square miles of rural Derbyshire, Staffordshire, Cheshire, Greater Manchester and West and South Yorkshire, is a good base for those who want to explore each part of this magnificent natural playground. It is a pretty village, overlooked by the imposing ruins of Peveril Castle and not far from the dramatic Winnats Pass. A superb round walk of about 5 miles

may be taken from the village up through the Pass and on to the summit of Mam Tor, the 'Shivering Mountain'.

North of Mam Tor and below Kinder Scout lies Edale, the starting-point of the Pennine Way. A large number of short waymarked walks begin here, and the village has an excellent information centre. A good way of seeing the northern part of the Park is to tackle a short stretch of the Way itself. If you make the ascent of Kinder Scout, however, do so with prudence and respect.

Bakewell, known as the capital of the Peak District, makes an excellent base and has a very good tourist office. Chatsworth and Haddon Hall are only a short distance away, and at Monsal Head there is a dramatic high spot where the Wye snakes through the gorge 200 feet below. You can hire cycles in Bakewell and elsewhere in the Peak Park as well; cycle touring is becoming increasingly popular and there are a number of cycle routes.

The main town on the eastern side of the Peak District is Buxton, which in fact lies outside the boundary of the Park. This is a fascinating spa town much visited by the Victorians, and its buildings still recall a more spacious

Panoramic outlook from Stanage Edge near Hathersage in the eastern part of the Peak District National Park. Climbers gather here to tackle the spectacular rock face.

age. The area between Buxton and Tideswell is well worth exploring. So too is the Goyt valley to the west, where roads are closed on Sundays and a one-way traffic scheme operates at other times. The walker can thus explore the fine wooded paths and deep rocky clefts of this beautiful river valley without fear of being run down.

For the Peak District at its widest and best, take the A57 cross Pennine road from Glossop via the Snake Pass and Lady Bower Reservoir to Hathersage. From here School Lane at the back of the village climbs up steeply, eventually reaching Stanage Edge, one of the rock-climbing meccas of the Peaks. There are top-of-the-world panoramas here, to Manchester in the west and Sheffield in the east, and fine hill walks everywhere.

Ashbourne is also the starting-point of the Tissington Trail, a 13-mile path along the route of the old branch line between Ashbourne and Buxton, a walk on which you simply cannot get

lost. Distant views alternate with deep cuttings. Tissington and nearby Hartington are quaint backwaters, most famous for the well-dressing ceremonies held each Ascension Day. At Parsley Hay, where there is a first-class camping-ground, the Tissington Trail meets an even more spectacular route, the High Peak Trail.

The High Peak Trail

This path follows the old Cromford and High Peak Railway from Cromford to Dowlow. The walker who completes the full 17 miles will pass through some of the most spectacular scenery Derbyshire has to offer. There are in addition many relics of the age of steam along the track.

The Cromford and High Peak Railway linked the Cromford Canal and Peak Forest Canals, transporting coal, iron and minerals to the industrial centres of the north and Midlands. It was built in the early 1830s at a total cost of £180,000.

There are a number of interesting features along the Trail. Lead was once mined at Brassington, and nearby, at Harboro' Rocks, the caves contain

traces of Stone Age settlements. When the railway was opened, the wagons had to be hauled up the steep Middleton Incline by a steam winding-engine that can still be seen in the Middleton Top Engine House. Black Rocks is popular with climbers, and there are attractive round walks through the nearby woods. Cromford Canal, a short distance away, is extremely attractive, and Cromford itself, where in 1771 Sir Richard Arkwright opened his first cotton mill, is also worth a visit.

Peak District walkers may also like to tackle two other major footpath routes through less well known country on the edge of the National Park.

The Gritstone Trail

To the east of Macclesfield the Cheshire hills rise abruptly to 1800 feet, curving round the county borders like a protecting arm. Through the heart of this fine region winds the 18-mile Gritstone Trail. The route begins at Lyme Park, a gracious estate now owned by the National Trust, and ends at Rushton on the Staffordshire border.

The Trail takes its name from the gritstone rocks thrust up through a massive crack in the earth's crust some 150 million years ago. The stone is made up of coarse angular fragments resembling grit and feels rough to the touch. It is often known as millstone grit, for it was once used for grinding corn.

The area has been worked industriously by man, and there is much evidence of quarrying and milling along the Trail. The route is also extremely attractive, especially at Sponds Hill, the northern starting-point, and at Tegg's Nose Country Park, the halfway point. The walker passes through open moorland, lush woodland, grazing farmland and one or two surprisingly wild and steep sections, notably on the descent from Croker Hill.

The Trail, which is well signposted, may be muddy in places in winter. Stout footwear is recommended.

The Staffordshire Way

The Staffordshire Way runs for 59 miles between Mow Cop, a little north-west of Stoke-on-Trent, and Cannock Chase, south-west of Stafford, through

some of the county's best scenery and several of its most interesting villages and towns. There are plans to extend the Way another 30 miles south to Kinder Edge, close to the great West Midlands conurbation.

The Way starts along the rugged gritstone of Congleton Edge, on the south-western side of the Peak District, and later descends to follow the towpath of the restored Caldon Canal through the secluded Churnet valley. Hill-top paths follow, giving dramatic views over the Staffordshire 'Rhineland', as the valley of the river Churnet is known.

From Rocester the Way follows the river Dove to the fine old market town of Uttoxeter and then runs through undulating farmland to Abbots Bromley, famous for its annual Horn Dance. There are wide views across Blithfield reservoir before the descent to Colton village and the Trent valley. Pleasant tow-path walking brings the route to a conclusion at Shugborough Hall, set in beautiful parkland on Cannock Chase. The Chase was once part of a vast royal hunting preserve that covered most of Staffordshire during the Middle Ages.

Above left Peveril Castle, built only two years after the Conquest and one of the first Norman castles for which stone was used. The present keep dates from a century later.

Top Railway viaduct at Monsal Dale. In the Peak District, as elsewhere, abandoned lines have been converted at relatively low cost into excellent walking routes.

Above Upper Dovedale looking towards the heights of the Peak District.

155

The Viking Way

The Viking Way—the name acknowledges the Scandinavian influence on England's eastern counties—runs for approximately 140 miles from the Humber Bridge to Oakham in Leicestershire. The route includes historical and geological features of interest, and naturalists and archaeologists will also find much to absorb them. The going is easy through an attractive but little-known and relatively unpopulated part of England's countryside; there are also remarkably few hills.

From the Humber Bridge, the Way runs southwards through the Lincolnshire Wolds, passing several villages of Danish origin and the Roman town of Caistor. It then follows the attractive gravel valley of the river Bain to Horncastle, from where it runs along a 7-mile section of disused railway track to Woodhall Spa. Now the Way turns westwards along the Witham valley on a riverside course to the cathedral city of Lincoln, which was one of the main towns of Roman Britain. Lincoln 'Cliff', a long limestone escarpment, follows, providing dramatic views westwards across the Trent valley.

The Way now traces the course of the Roman Ermine Street across the once-wild and desolate Ancaster Heath and then turns west again, along the valley of the Upper Witham, the prehistoric Sewstern Lane and, for a short distance, the Grantham Canal. It continues through Leicestershire to Oakham via Rutland Water, Britain's largest man-made reservoir.

For most of its distance the Viking Way follows public footpaths, bridleways and green lanes, but there are some short sections of road walking.

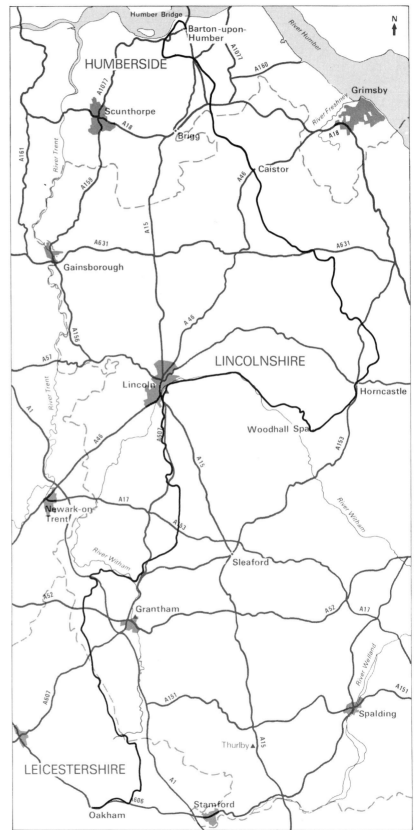

The Yorkshire Dales National Park

Although the beautiful 680-square-mile Dales National Park is sometimes considered the gentler of Yorkshire's two National Parks, it boasts several peaks of over 2000 feet, higher than any summit in its neighbour. These high fells form part of the great watershed of England. Many of the streams that rise among the limestone scars descend through rocky gorges as rushing waterfalls to swell the rivers of the Dales. Add the massive gritstone heights of the mountain peaks and the broad pastoral valleys and you have an area with a strong appeal.

Many of the Dales' best-known and most fascinating spots fall along the Pennine Way, which cuts straight across the Park from south to north. There are, however, a number of other areas well worth the walker's attention.

On the eastern side of the park, between Grassington and Aysgarth, the footpaths of Wharfedale provide plentiful fine walks. Three especially enjoyable ones lead from Bolton Abbey to the celebrated high point of Simon's Seat, from Buckden along the old Roman road to Yockenthwaite, and from Kettlewell to Arncliffe, recommended if dramatic views are your objective.

On the western side of the Park are two giant and very distinctive summits, Whernside and Ingleborough. These, together with the more central Pen-y-Ghent, which lies on the Pennine Way, form the famous Three Peaks, all well over 2000 feet high. The Three Peaks have been a target for walkers ever since 1887, when two schoolmasters scaled the trio in some fourteen hours. Since then the Three Peaks Walk has become steadily more popular and competitive. In 1960 Frank Dawson of Salford was the first to achieve the 'circuit' in less than three hours. The shortest distances between the summits are 7¼ miles, 4½ and 8¾ miles: complete that within a long summer day, and you really can call yourself an accomplished fell walker.

The Ebor Way and The Dales Way

Two medium-distance recreational paths in Yorkshire run through some really magnificent terrain and offer some of the best of both low- and high-country walking in Britain.

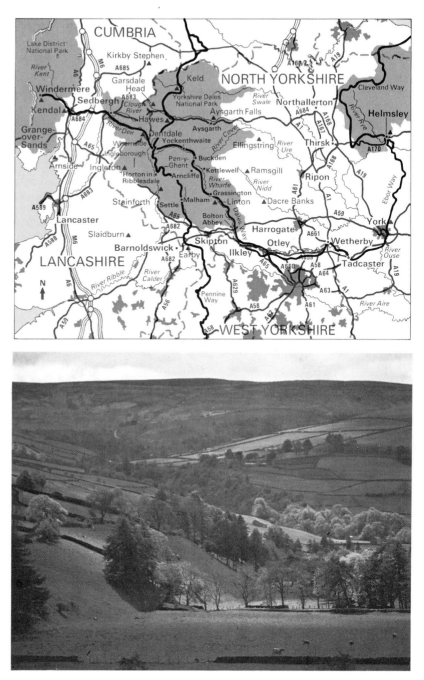

The Ebor Way starts at Helmsley–also one of the end-points of the Cleveland Way–and traces a fairly gentle 70-mile route right across the fertile Vale of York. It passes through the historic city of York and then runs through Tadcaster and Wetherby to Harewood. West of Wetherby, the Way gradually ascends, following the strongly-etched landscape of Wharfedale to Ilkley, the most famous of the Yorkshire hill towns. From Ilkley the

Sweeping slopes make for energetic and invigorating walking in the Yorkshire Dales.

Dales Way runs across the Pennines for a further 80 miles roughly north-west to Windermere in the Lake District. This is a regal, infinitely rewarding, and fairly arduous footpath.

157

The North York Moors National Park

In addition to the Cleveland Way, which more or less completely encircles it, the North York Moors National Park offers some grand walking. This is a landscape of wide horizons and regal, high moorland, split and softened by beautiful narrow valleys and dotted with villages and hamlets as pretty as they are permanent and solid.

Hutton-le-Hole on the southern flank of the high moors is proudly–and rightly–proclaimed as the prettiest village in all Yorkshire. The Ryedale Folk Museum there has a fascinating collection of reconstructed dwellings and equipment. To the north-east of Hutton-le-Hole the heights around Rosedale Abbey are very impressive, yet relatively undiscovered. There is a pleasant camping-ground here, a first-class base for walks along the banks of the rushing Seven and northwards to the lonely sweeps of Egton and Wester-dale Moors. On the western side of the Park, Hawnby is another tiny hamlet in a quite magnificent setting, reached by a minor road from Osmotherley through some inspiring scenery.

The moors are by no means bleak and featureless, and there is a wealth of forest across the uplands. The Pickering District Forest, administered by the Forestry Commission, is some 24,000 hectares large and is sub-divided into no less than six separate forests. One of the most impressive of these is Cropton. The Spiers House camping-ground is in a most pleasant spot in the heart of this conifer plantation. There are some good waymarked forest walks quite literally on the doorstep.

Walkers very quickly fall in love with the North Yorkshire Moors–the love affair usually lasts a lifetime–and sooner or later the famous Lyke Wake Walk must be tackled. The Walk runs across the windswept, desolate moors for 40 miles at their highest and widest, from Scarth Wood Moor above Osmother-ley to Ravenscar on the coast. Real enthusiasts try to complete the course, which is an arduous trek even in the best of weather, in twenty-four hours, and some 3000 succeed every year.

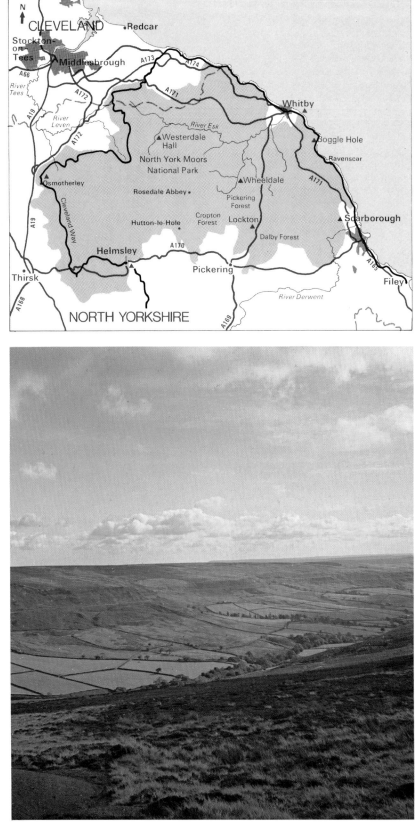

Rosedale Head, North Yorkshire, from Blekley Ridge.

The Forest of Bowland

Practically ignored by the holiday crowds rushing northwards to the Lake District, the Forest of Bowland is a landscape scarcely altered since the Industrial Revolution. The name is somewhat inapt, for the Forest is now 300 square miles of grand moorland. Its geology is similar to that of the Pennines, from which it is separated by the green Ribble valley. The high plateaus of these gritstone fells and scarps are divided by a number of beautiful, secret dales that contain many delightful wooded, waterside walks. In Littledale and Swyredale you can walk all day and hardly see another soul, even in high summer.

Another virtue of Bowland is that few roads run through the Forest. In the central part, where there are no major roads, the villages and hamlets are tiny and scattered. This is one of the few places left in England where you will find true country silence.

In the south of the Forest, Beacon Hill, only eight miles from Preston, is a popular walk with magnificent views at the end. More adventurous visitors will enjoy the magnificent footpaths from Chipping, an attractive village huddled around an old church, over Wolf Fell and Fair Oak Fell.

Even practised walkers should remember to treat the Forest of Bowland with the respect it deserves. There is some very stern terrain and away from the popular beauty spots the paths are not well marked.

Forest of Bowland landscape. Here the walker may tramp undisturbed through pleasant valleys and over exhilarating moorland heights.

The Lake District National Park

The wooded slopes of Grasmere, one of the more popular lakes. There is pleasant walking around the shore.

This country is England at her most beautiful. Scarcely 50 miles across at the widest point, the 866 square-mile National Park encompasses almost 200 peaks, over 60 lakes and many valleys of sublime beauty.

But why should anyone want to visit the Lake District in high summer? The area is grossly overcrowded, the twisting, narrow roads are choked with traffic and accommodation is hard to find. On top of all this, Seathwaite Farm, 8 miles from Keswick, is the wettest inhabited spot in Britain.

Nowadays it is only the walker who can capture the exhilarating magic of the Lake District. For those prepared to use their feet, the Lakeland that inspired poets such as Wordsworth and Ruskin is still there unchanged, a miracle of landscape that might have been formed with the hill-walker in mind.

The Lake District may be compact, but, as most visitors know, it is also complex, and it takes time to understand its geography. First-time visitors may therefore find it an advantage to explore a particular locality rather than to try to take in the whole of the National Park.

An unofficial dividing line runs between the southern and northern parts of the Park. In the south there is Windermere, Grasmere, Ambleside and Coniston; all but Ambleside have nearby waters named after them. Keswick is at the centre of the northern district. To the west and east are Cockermouth and Penrith, both just outside the boundary of the Park. Between them lie the sparkling lakes of Bassenthwaite, Derwentwater and Ullswater. Separating the two great valleys is the real high-country, dominated by Helvellyn, Scafell Pike (at 3210 feet England's highest mountain) and Shap.

The most popular and most congested area is the rough triangle formed by Windermere, Grasmere and Coniston. This is tourist Lakeland, cluttered but pretty. Windermere, the largest and busiest lake, bustles with pleasure boats, and Grasmere is invariably crowded with pilgrims making for Wordsworth's cottage. There are some pleasant, easy walks from the western side of Windermere between Hawkshead and the lake shore. Round-the-lake walks are popular too, for there are no route-finding problems and the going is fairly easy.

Buttermere, Wast Water, Crummock, Grasmere and Loweswater are some of the shorter circuits (4 to 7 miles); Derwent Water, Haweswater and Coniston are longer.

It is the high-level tracks that provide the real reward, however, and all serious walkers will sooner or later be pulled towards the towering trio of Scafell, Scafell Pike and Great Gable. To get there you drive west from Ambleside on a minor road that winds heavenwards over Wrynose and Hard Knott Passes and then plummets down to Eskdale and the terminus of the famous miniature railway. You then back-track via Santon Bridge to the end of the road at Wasdale Head, where there is a camping-ground and a hotel.

Wasdale Head is a good base from which to tackle a variety of hill tracks as dramatic as any in western Europe. Although most of the paths are clearly defined and not too strenuous, at least on the lower slopes, novices should not try to tackle summits on their own or in poor weather. When the weather is fine, however, and you are in the right company, this best of Lake District hill-walking.

Another firm favourite, only a little less stern and almost as majestic, is Helvellyn and the renowned Striding Edge, a sky-scraping razor's-edge path. The 3-mile climb (which, again, should not be attempted on a sudden whim) starts from a parking area about halfway between Keswick and Grasmere, alongside the A591. In fine weather the views are breathtaking.

The natural attraction near Keswick, a picturesque town and a good shopping centre, is Derwent Water. There is a large camping-site right on the shore, where canoeing and other water sports are easily available. As always, the surroundings are beautiful, the headwaters of the Derwent flowing through Borrowdale, which many consider to be the outstanding Lakeland valley.

On the eastern side of the National Park the road from Windermere to Ullswater winds over Kirkstone Pass, the highest in the Lake District, 1500 feet above sea level. On the way to Patterdale, at the southern end of the lake, it passes Brothers Water. There is a pub and a camping-ground here and another superb walking area close to Ullswater, perhaps the most beautiful of the great lakes.

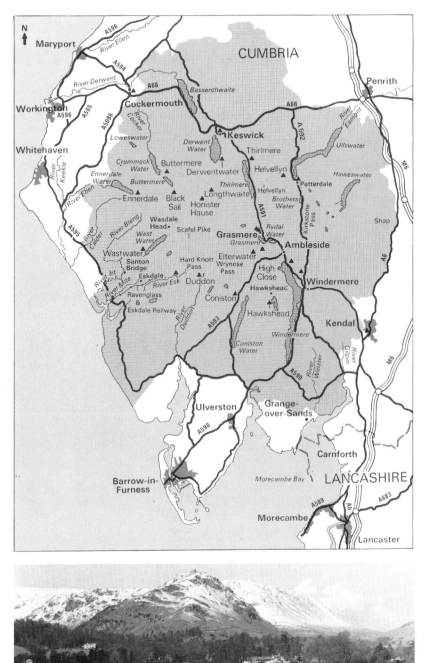

Winter view across Grasmere towards the Lake District peaks, at other seasons a mecca for walkers and climbers.

Northumberland National Park

Kielder Forest, where some 145,000 acres have been planted during the past half century. Forest rides and paths provide pleasant walks here.

Stretching across some 40 miles of hill-country, from Hadrian's Wall to the Cheviots, the Northumberland National Park contains 398 square miles of truly wild and isolated beauty: not for nothing is Northumberland sometimes called 'the forgotten county'. This frontier region, much of which has changed little since Roman times, has had a very turbulent history. At Otterburn you can visit the site of the moonlit battle between the English and the Scots in 1388. Northumbria was the last to accept the King's Peace after the union of 1603, and today it retains a proud independence.

The classic route from the south is along the A1(M) and then the A68 through the increasingly attractive Durham countryside and on to Hexham, just below the Wall. The picturesque town is steeped in history and makes one of the best starting-points for any Northumberland visit. There is a good information office in the centre and a pleasant camping-ground near the racecourse 1½ miles above the town.

Hexham is close to all the principal Roman sites, from Corbridge and Chesters in the east to Housesteads, Steel Rigg and Walltown Crags west-wards. At Vindolands, there is an impressive frontier fort and settlement; many exciting discoveries have been made here and work is still in progress. For one of the most revealing short walks along the Wall, take the B6318 from Greenhead, just west of Halt-whistle, and then the minor road to Cawfields. From here you can walk for some 8 miles to the highly dramatic viewpoint above Crag Lough. Early in the day is the most atmospheric time.

The natural attractions of England's northernmost National Park are con-siderable and varied. In the central area the heather-covered sandstone Simonside hills between Otterburn and Rothbury contrast with the wooded slopes of the rivers Coquet, Rede and Tyne. Both provide superb walking for the visitor. From Bellingham there is an easy stroll out of the town up the steep-sided valley of Hareshaw Burn to Hareshaw Linn, one of the county's prettiest waterfalls.

The Border forests–those in Northumberland are Kielder, Falstone, Wark and Redesdale–are one of the biggest man-made plantations in Europe. Ample car-parks, picnic areas and camping-grounds enable the visitor to explore the forests on foot. Some of the roads too are still a pleasure to drive on, among them the Forest Drive from Kielder to Byrness, which passes through remote forest and moorland. In the heart of the forest is the massive Kielder Water Scheme which, when completed, will be the largest man-made lake in Europe. The North Tyne valley will be totally transformed–but not at the expense of the outdoor enthusiast, we are assured, for whom many facilities, including nature trails, will be provided. An information centre near Falstone, at Yarrow Moor, has some interesting displays.

During the summer, the Park authorities operate a full-time warden

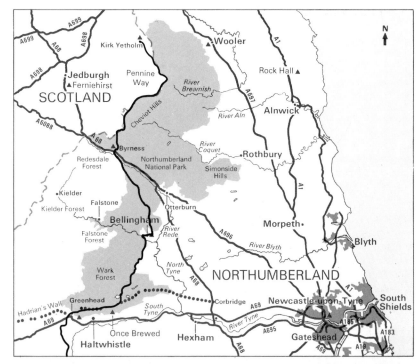

service to help and advise visitors. A programme of over 250 guided walks of every length and on every theme is available from the information office at Hexham. If you prefer to go it alone, remember that only experienced hill-walkers well versed in map and com-pass work should tackle the lengthier and more remote paths.

The view east along Hadrian's Wall just west of Housesteads. The Pennine Way runs along this stretch of what was once the outermost edge of the Roman Empire.

Scotland

Sooner or later, all true hill-walkers will find themselves making for the heather hills north of the Border. Here, where Britain's highest mountain towers and lakes become lochs and valleys glens, is a wild and regal land. Space makes it impossible to describe all the outstandingly beautiful walking areas the country has to offer. The three suggestions made here are no more than appetite-whetters, intended to stimulate you to further exploration of your own.

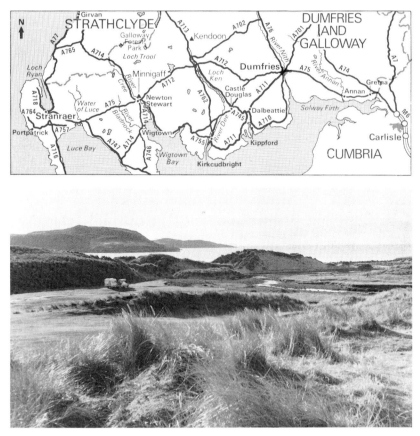

Galloway

This land of Burns and Robert the Bruce is a Highlands in miniature, a corner scarcely less dramatic than the land further north. The immediate impression once you have turned westwards along the Solway is of tranquility, space and a grand landscape of majestic forests and granite hills. The coast is always dramatic and often outstanding, as the coastal paths near Gatehouse-on-Fleet and Portpatrick prove. The charming little harbours are still blessedly free of the oppressive crowding that afflicts so many English resorts in summer.

The great magnet for the walker, however, is the Galloway Forest Park above Newton Stewart. The camping-ground at Caldons on the shore of Loch Trool is an excellent base. Here you really are away from it all, surrounded by miles of forest plantations and magnificent hills. A waymarked forest trail circles the beautiful little loch nestling amid a cluster of wooded, lofty peaks. Bruce's Stone north of the loch commemorates the ancient hero, who in 1306 started his guerilla campaign here against the English. Merrick, at 2770 feet the highest peak in southern Scotland, can be ascended via the Buchan Burn track on the northern shore of the loch. It is a superb walk but a strenuous one and should not be undertaken lightly.

The Cairngorm mountains

In the heart of the Cairngorms, Loch Morlich and Glen More are another magnificent landscape for the walker. There is a well-run conifer-sheltered forestry camping-ground here, open all the year round, from where the walker may choose from a host of trails, short and long, easy and strenuous, amid forest and high mountain peaks. There

is an information centre at Glenmore Lodge where a variety of outdoor pursuits for organized groups or individuals is available, including canoeing, climbing, skiing and nature rambles.

One celebrated walk—but one only to be tackled by the experienced—is the 30-mile marathon from Aviemore to Braemar through the Lairig Ghru Pass. Here one could well be in Austria or Switzerland, so majestic are the mountains, Ben Macdhui on one side and Cairn Toul on the other, both well over 4200 feet high. Cairngorm itself is the baby of the mighty trio at 4084 feet. This is a two-day hike; you can either

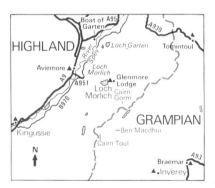

camp or spend the night in a mountain bothy such as Sinclair's Hut.

There are of course countless gentler walks throughout the vast forest park between Loch Morlich and Aviemore and numerous other interesting areas to explore. At Loch Garten, for instance, you might have the good fortune to spot one of the jealously-guarded ospreys.

Gair Loch

The splintered and rugged Western Highland coast would take a lifetime to explore properly. One especially beautiful area is around Gair Loch (not to be confused with the nuclear submarine base at Gare Loch in the south). Some three miles west of the little town of Gairloch is a magnificent camping-ground, set in what must be one of the most scenic spots in Europe. Sandy beaches, splendid panoramas and spectacular sunsets await the visitor.

Not far from here, from the pretty village of Shieldaig on Loch Torridon, you can walk among some of Scotland's finest hills and forests, where stags abound and sea otters cavort in the

clear waters of the lochs. In early autumn the landscape is a riot of colour.

When your feet need a rest, drive from Shieldaig to Applecross via the Pass of the Cattle (Bealach na Ba). This is one of the most spectacular roads in Britain which takes you over a summit of well over 2000 feet before descending to the white-painted fishing cottages of Applecross.

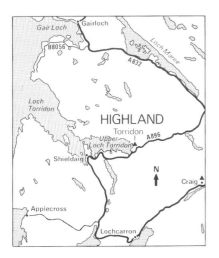

Opposite The wide, exhilarating shore of Gair Loch. Here there is fishing, swimming and walking and truly regal scenery.

Top Loch Morlich, 1000 feet high, near Aviemore in the Cairngorm Mountains. Reindeer–brought in thirty years ago from Lapland–wander here among the trees.

Above Loch Trool Forest Park, where there is fine walking amid the so-called Galloway 'Highlands' of southern Scotland.

Walking Within the Law

The walker's legal obligations are few, simple, clear-cut and largely a matter of common sense. All the long-distance footpaths described in this book, together with the selection mentioned in The Best of British Walks and the gazetteers, are public rights of way. The term is self-explanatory. The law gives you the right to walk on all the 100,000 miles or more of Britain's public footpaths. Where such paths are also bridleways, you may also cycle along them or ride on a horse.

However, your rights apply only to the public path or bridleway itself, not to adjacent land, whether this is fenced or open–a finer point of law sometimes ignored or misunderstood. Every square foot of the country, including the National Parks, is owned by an individual or a public authority, and there is no such thing as 'common' land. Even though a path crosses wild, remote country, the walker does not have free access to camp, light fires, pick flowers or leave rubbish. This is important on fells and open moorland: it is crucial in farmland and forests.

If a farm gate has a 'keep closed' notice, it is nothing short of criminal to ignore the request, even if grazing animals are not obvious. And to let your dog chase sheep is not only indictable, in hill-farm country, where farmers may respond to such behaviour with a shot gun, it may cost your pet its life.

Not all paths are clear and precisely signposted, and sometimes the walker will find himself confronted with an impenetrable jungle of undergrowth or a field of waving corn where the map clearly indicates a path. Here we enter a complex and uncertain area of the law. A landowner must by law keep public rights of way clear of obstructions; if he does not cut back intrusive undergrowth, the local authority is empowered to do so and to charge him for the service. However, this is hardly an immediate comfort to the walker. The case is similar with fields of wheat. If he has given prior notice a farmer may in some cases sow or plough over a path, provided he restores the right of way within a given time.

If a path definitely does pass through a field of wheat, the walker may follow it, causing as little damage as possible.

In practice, of course, few people have the heart or the nerve to do this. By making a detour, however, perhaps around the edge of the field, they commit trespass. All one can do in such circumstances is to use intelligence and care and, should a confrontation arise, understanding rather than belligerence. In most cases this works well enough.

Some obstructions–such as bulls– are not so easy to negotiate. Local by-laws vary. It is sometimes necessary for the farmer to graze bulls over land crossed by recognized footpaths, and notices are not always displayed. A wary eye, agility and circumspection are needed here and, needless to say, neither children nor elderly people should walk near the animal. Never underestimate the bull, for he kills a number of people every year.

Safety First

There are of course no legal obligations on walkers to take care of themselves in remote hill country, any more than there are on small-boat sailors. If you want to behave with suicidal rashness, no law can stop you. But you are under a moral obligation to avoid putting your potential rescuers at needless risk, and for this reason alone you must take all reasonable precautions.

Never set out to walk a strange hill path on a whim. Each expedition should be properly prepared. Do not walk alone until and unless you are fully experienced, proficient with map and compass and know your physical and mental limitations.

Even so, solo walking over terrain away from recognized, frequented footpaths can be fraught with hazards. Two people are always company. Three are even better: in case of accident, one can stay with the injured person while the other goes for help.

But there is no need to be timorous or inflexible. Obviously, a summer walk on the South Downs is very different from a strenuous winter crossing of Kinder Scout, and you will quickly learn the difference. None the less, if you do err, let it be on the side of caution. Never treat any hill country, no matter how benign it may appear in the sunshine, with anything other than real respect, and always be prepared for the worst. The weather can change with alarming suddenness at high levels, transforming the tops into a freezing white hell while in the valleys below all

is serene. Remember that, climatically, 3000 feet up in Britain is equivalent to 8000 amid the Alps. Mid-winter weather can swirl around Snowdon or Ben Nevis even in high summer.

Distances stretch in the hills, and a long and arduous walk may be necessary to reach a road or habitation that appears just a short way off. And once your energy begins to drain, it does so at an alarming rate. In consequence, the right clothing and equipment, way-finding expertise, fitness and knowledge of how to behave in an emergency are vital factors in serious hill-walking.

Never set off in the mountains without notifying someone of your destination and when you intend to return. As a last–rather than a first– resort, leave a note taped to the inside of your car windscreen, with details of timing and objective. It is far better, though, to notify a park warden, the police or someone at your base.

Carry the standard emergency survival gear–extra warm clothing, means of providing a hot drink, fast-calory food such as Kendal Mint Cake or chocolate, a first-aid kit, torch and whistle. With these last you can give the standard distress warning in the hills, six flashes or blasts.

If you do find yourself in real trouble, either because of injury or exhaustion, stop, take stock, take action. Most of the deaths in Britain's mountain regions (there are over 200 each year) are caused by exposure (more commonly called hypothermia) aggravated by ignorance or fear. Fear is perhaps the greatest killer of all, simply because, consumed by fright, people find it almost impossible to think straight or take the right actions.

The natural inclination (sometimes extremely difficult to resist) is to rush down the mountain regardless. This is the very worst thing you could do. Stay put: make yourself snug, in a nest of bracken if possible, out of the wind. Put all your clothing on, including waterproofs, even though it may not be raining, eat some of your quick-energy food, and wait. Sooner or later rescuers will arrive. That thought should help to sustain you and to dispel the most dangerous threat in any mountain emergency, fear itself.

Fortunately, only a tiny minority gets into really serious trouble. So long as you behave responsibly you will roam the high country for a lifetime without a real moment of crisis.

The Country Code

All country walkers should abide by the Country Code. Its few rules are simple, and by rigidly observing them we help to preserve the countryside and an atmosphere of trust between town and country dwellers.

Guard against all risk of fire
A carelessly thrown match or cigarette-end could start an inferno, especially in forests at dry seasons. Never light a cooking fire when camping without express permission to do so.

Fasten all gates
This should be automatic; even if you find a farm gate open, close it behind you. It can take hours to recover a straying animal which can damage itself or growing crops or cause a serious road accident.

Keep dogs under control
Dogs should be put on a lead whenever requested and always when crossing sheep-grazing land and during the lambing season. A wayward dog almost always signifies an irresponsible owner. Make sure both you and your pet are properly trained to wander the countryside.

Keep to rights of way across farmland
Crops are valuable and are not always instantly identifiable as such: what may look like grass may be precious clover or young wheat.

Avoid damaging fences, hedges and walls
If you do have to force your way through a fence or hedge, do so as delicately as possible. If you inadvertently dislodge a dry stone wall in hill country, repair it before moving on.

Leave no litter
This is a slovenly, unsociable and dangerous habit. Plastic bags choke cattle and tin cans and bottles will slash paws, hooves and tendons. Take your litter home with you or to a litter basket.

Safeguard water supplies
Never pollute flowing streams with waste matter or detergent. All our drinking water comes from country streams and reservoirs, so keep them pure.

Protect wild life, plants and trees
The ecology of the countryside is delicately balanced. Do not disturb the fine interweave of animal and plant life by picking flowers, uprooting trees or killing or frightening wild creatures.

Go carefully on country roads
These are working routes for farmers. If a tractor or a flock of sheep blocks your way or slows you down, show patience and courtesy: you are the interloper.

Respect the life of the countryside
For the countryman, the landscape is an open-air workshop, and farm machinery and implements are often left unattended. Allay the traditional suspicion of country people for town dwellers by considerate and responsible behaviour.

Recreational Paths

As well as the nine long-distance footpaths described earlier in this book, an extensive country-wide network of Recreational Paths awaits the walker. Most of these paths have been established by local authorities; on many waymarking and maintenance work is carried out by volunteers.

These short and medium-distance paths are designed to appeal both to families in search of an afternoon's stroll and to more serious walkers. Most of them are routed across fairly gentle country, though the walking is none the less enjoyable for that. A few, such as The Calderdale Way and The Dales Way, are fairly strenuous in parts.

The list below gives brief details of many of the Recreational Paths recognized by the Countryside Commission. Some of these are described in greater detail in the appropriate section of *The Best of British Walks*.

The figure in brackets indicates the length of the path in miles. The figure in bold indicates the relevant Ordnance Survey map number.

PATH NAME	ADDRESS FOR INFORMATION	DESCRIPTION
ENGLAND		
Avon		
Avon Walkway (27) **172**	Bristol Information Centre, Colston House, Bristol BS1 5AQ	Follows the river Avon from Pill, through the Avon Gorge and the centre of Bristol along the Avon valley via Bath to Dundas Aqueduct on Kennet and Avon Canal.
Cotswold Way – see Gloucestershire		
West Mendip Way – see Somerset		
Buckinghamshire		
North Buckingham-shire Way (30) **152, 165**	Ramblers' Association, 1–5 Wandsworth Road, London SW8 2LJ	From Chequers Knap on the northern scarp of the Chiltern hills through the Vale of Aylesbury to Wolverton, where it joins the Grafton Way.
Cambridge		
Wimpole Way (11)	Cambridgeshire County Council, Shire Hall, Cambridge CB3 0AP	From Cambridge city centre south-west to the National Trust estate at Wimpole.
Cheshire		
Gritstone Trail (17) **109, 118**	Cheshire County Council, Countryside and Recreation Division, County Hall, Chester CH1 1SF	From Lyme Park, a National Trust country park, to Rushton, where it links with the Staffordshire Way.
Sandstone Trail (30) **117**	Cheshire County Council, Countryside and Recreation Division, County Hall, Chester CH4 1SF	Beacon Hill, Frodsham, to Grindley Brook on the borders of Shropshire.
Wirral Way* (18) **108, 117**	Head Ranger, Wirral Country Park, Thurstaston Visitor Centre, Station Road, Thurstaston, Wirral L67 0HN	West Kirby to Hooton through Wirral Country Park (not suitable for cyclists).
Cumbria		
Dales Way (81) **90, 97, 98**	Dalesman Publishing Co. Ltd, Clapham (via Lancaster), North Yorkshire LA2 8EB	A difficult path from Ilkley to Bowness on Lake Windermere, following the rivers Wharfe, Dee, Lune and Kent. It crosses, and for a short distance follows, the Pennine Way long-distance path.

PATH NAME	ADDRESS FOR INFORMATION	DESCRIPTION
Derbyshire		
Cal-der-went Walk (30) **110**	Dalesman Publishing Co. Ltd, Clapham (via Lancaster), North Yorkshire LA2 8EB *The Cal-der-went Walk* by Geoffrey Carr	From the river Calder at Harbury Bridge, Wakefield, to the river Derwent at Ladybower Reservoir in Peak National Park, crossing the watersheds and valleys of the rivers Dearne, Don and Porter.
High Peak Trail* (17) **119**	Peak District National Park, Aldern House, Baslow Road, Bakewell, Derbyshire DE4 1AE	Follows the old Cromford and High Peak Railway through fine scenery from Cromford to Dowlow, connecting with the Tissington Trail at Parsley Hay and Middleton Top.
Tissington Trail* (13) **119**	Peak District National Park, Aldern House, Baslow Road, Bakewell, Derbyshire DE4 1AE	Follows the old Buxton–Ashbourne railway line from Ashbourne to Parsley Hay, where it connects with the High Peak Trail, through fine, varied scenery.
Durham		
Bishop Brandon Walk (10) **88, 92, 93**	Durham County Council, County Planning Dept, County Hall, Durham DH1 5UF	From Bishop Auckland across the river Wear on the Newton Cab viaduct, through farmland and along Wear valley to Broompark picnic site.
Deerness Valley Walk (7) **88, 92**	Durham County Council, County Planning Dept, County Hall, Durham DH1 5UE	From Broompark picnic site along the Deerness valley towards Crook.
Derwent Walk (10) **88**	Durham County Council, County Planning Dept, County Hall, Durham DH1 5UE	Swalwell on Tyneside to Blackhill near Consett. Part of a 300-acre country park with riverside picnic area, woodlands and attractive views of Derwent valley.
Wear Valley Way (46) **87, 92, 93**	45 Moorland Close, Sunnybrow, Crook, Co. Durham DL15 0BX	A strenuous, high-level walk from Killhope to Willington, originally envisaged as a 24-hour walk, now divided in 9 sections.
East Sussex		
Forest Way* (10) **187, 188**	East Sussex County Council, County Planning Dept, Southover House, Southover Road, Lewes, East Sussex	Groomsbridge to East Grinstead through Forest Way County Park.
Sussex Border Path (148) **186, 187, 188, 189, 197, 198, 199**	A. Mackintosh, 253 Hawthorn Road, Bognor Regis, Sussex and Dr B. Perkins, 11 Old London Road, Patcham, Brighton, Sussex *The Sussex Border Path*	Follows the Sussex border from Emsworth to Rye, also the East and West Sussex border from East Grinstead to Southwick. A link route connects Rye with the South Downs Way.
Wealdway (26)	Tunbridge Wells Rambling Club, c/o G. King, Fox House, Hadlow Stair, Tonbridge, Kent	Gravesend to Eastbourne with fine view of surrounding countryside, connecting with the Saxon Shore Way and the South Downs Way.
Essex		
Essex Way (50) **167, 168, 177**	East Anglia Tourist Board, 14 Museum Street, Ipswich IP1 1HU	Epping to Dedham in the beautiful Constable country.
Forest Way (20)	Essex County Council, County Hall, Chelmsford CM1 1CF	Epping Forest to Hatfield Forest following ancient roads and tracks and linking several large, attractive areas of open space.

PATH NAME	ADDRESS FOR INFORMATION	DESCRIPTION
Gloucestershire		
Cotswold Way (100) **151, 162, 163, 172**	Thornhill Press, 24 Moorend Road, Cheltenham, Glos. *The Cotswold Way* by M. Richards. R. A. Long, 27 Lambert Avenue, Shurdington, Cheltenham, Glos. *Cotswold Way Handbook*	From Chipping Campden along the scarp edge of the Cotswold hills to Bath; panoramic views.
Oxfordshire Way – see Oxfordshire		
Wychavon Way – see Hereford and Worcester		
Hereford and Worcester		
Lower Wye Valley Walk – see Gwent		
North Worcestershire Footpath (19) **138, 139**	Hereford and Worcester County Council, County Estates Surveyor, Farrier House, Farrier Street, Worcester WR1 3EW	From Kingsford County Park to Lickey Hills south of Birmingham, passing through Waseley and Glent Country Parks.
Staffordshire and Worcestershire Canal Footpath (9)	Wyre Forest District Council, Director of Planning and Architectural Services, Land Oak House, Kidderminster, Hereford and Worcester DY10 1TA	North from Stourport through Kidderminster to Caunsall.
Wychavon Way (40) **150**	Wychavon District Council, Planning Dept, Norbury House, Friar Street, Droitwich, Worcs. WR9 8EG	From Holt Fleet on river Severn to Winchcombe where it joins Cotswold Way, then through attractive lowland countryside to Bredon Hill in Cotswold Area of Outstanding Natural Beauty and on to the Cotswold Hills.
Humberside		
Beverley 20 (20) **106, 107**	Director of Technical Services, Humberside County Council, Eastgate, Beverley, North Humberside	Called Beverley 20 because it is a 20-mile walk from Beverley Minster to the Humber Bridge.
Derwent Way (81) **100, 101, 105**	Dalesman Publishing Co. Ltd, Clapham (via Lancaster), North Yorkshire LA2 8EB *The Derwent Way* by R. C. Kenchington	From Barmby on the Marsh to Lilla Howe where it crosses the Lyke Wake Walk, via Kirkham Priory and Malton, following the river Derwent as closely as possible.
Minster Way (51)	Dr G. Eastwood, 60 Front Street, Lockington, Driffield, East Yorkshire *The Minster Way*	From Beverley Minster to York Minster through gentle and varied countryside.
Viking Way – see Lincolnshire		
Isle of Wight		
Bembridge Trail (15) **196**	Isle of Wight County Council, County Surveyor, County Hall, Newport, Isle of Wight PO31 1UD	Shide, near Newport, to Bembridge Point; down, marsh and woodland.
Coastal Path (60) **196**	Isle of Wight County Council, County Surveyor, County Hall, Newport, Isle of Wight PO31 1UD	A circuit of the coastline.
Hamstead Trail (8) **196**	Isle of Wight County Council, County Surveyor, County Hall, Newport, Isle of Wight PO31 1UD	Hamstead Ledge to Brooke Bay; starts on saltings near Newton Creek and runs over downland to Coastal Path.
Nunwell Trail (10) **196**	Isle of Wight County Council, County Surveyor, County Hall, Newport, Isle of Wight PO31 1UD	St John's station, Ryde, to Sandown station; mixed country route with downland and water meadows, passing Nunwell House.
Shepherds Trail (10) **196**	Isle of Wight County Council, County Surveyor, County Hall, Newport, Isle of Wight PO31 1UD	Whitcombe Cross, Carisbrooke, to Shepherds Chine, Atherfield; downland and scenic views, with several old manor houses on or near route.
Stenbury Trail (10) **196**	Isle of Wight County Council, County Surveyor, County Hall, Newport, Isle of Wight PO31 1UD	Blackwater, near Newport, to Coastal Path at St Lawrence, near Ventnor; river valley and downland; passes near Worsley Monument and Appuldurcombe House.
Tennyson Trail (15) **196**	Isle of Wight County Council, County Surveyor, County Hall, Newport, Isle of Wight PO31 1UD	Carisbrooke (near the castle) to Alum Bay via Tennyson Down; downland, forests and marine views.
Worsley Trail (15) **196**	Isle of Wight County Council, County Surveyor, County Hall, Newport, Isle of Wight PO31 1UD	Shanklin Old Village to Brighstone Forest, through pine forest, high countryside and downland and villages of historic and scenic importance; passes near Worsley Monument and Appuldurcombe House.
Kent		
Saxon Shore Way (140) **177, 178, 179, 189**	Kent Rights of Way Council, Lion Yard, Lewson Street, Sittingbourne, Kent ME9 9JS	Follows the Kent coast from Gravesend to Rye, coinciding in places with the North Downs Way and passing through four Roman forts and many other historic sites. Extensions are planned to Eastbourne and through East Anglia to the Norfolk coast.
Leicestershire		
Jubilee Way (16) **129, 130**	Leicestershire County Council, County Planning Dept, County Hall, Glenfield, Leicester	From Melton Mowbray through gently undulating countryside to Brewer's Gate, east of Woolsthorpe, where it links with the Viking Way.
Viking Way – see Lincolnshire		
Lincolnshire		
Jubilee Way – see Leicestershire		
Viking Way (140) **141, 112**	Lincolnshire County Council, County Offices, Lincoln LN1 1YL	From Oakham to the Humber Bridge, incorporating the short Spa Trail from Horncastle to Woodhall Spa.
Merseyside		
Wirral Way – see Cheshire		
Norfolk		
Weavers Way (15)	Norfolk County Council, County Hall, Martineau Lane, Norwich NR1 2DH	From Blickling to Statham.
Northamptonshire		
Grafton Way (12) **152**	Northamptonshire County Council, Leisure and Libraries Dept, Northampton House, Northampton NN1 2JP	Wolverton, where it links with the North Bucks Way, to Greens Norton, where it links with the Knightly Way.
Knightly Way (12) **152**	Northamptonshire County Council, Leisure and Libraries Dept, Northampton House, Northampton NN1 2JP	Greens Norton, where it links with the Grafton Way, to Badby.

RECREATIONAL PATHS

PATH NAME	ADDRESS FOR INFORMATION	DESCRIPTION
North Yorkshire		
Dales Way – see Cumbria		
Derwent Way – see Humberside		
Ebor Way (70) **100, 104, 105**	Dalesman Publishing Co. Ltd, Clapham (via Lancaster), North Yorkshire LA2 8EB *The Ebor Way* by J. K. E. Piggin	From Helmsley to Ilkley via York, linking the Cleveland Way long-distance path and the Dales Way.
Foss Walk (28) **100, 105**	N. G. Fife, River Foss Amenity Society, 77 Millfield Lane, Nether Poppleton, York YO2 6NA	A walk along the river Foss from York to Easingwold.
Lyke Wake Walk (40) **93, 94, 100, 101**	Dalesman Publishing Co. Ltd, Clapham (via Lancaster), North Yorkshire LA2 8EB *Lyke Wake Walk* by Bill Cowley	A strenuous walk across the North Yorkshire moors from Osmotherley to Ravenscar. Originally planned as a 24-hour timed walk; links with the Derwent Way.
North Wolds Walk (20)	North Wolds Walk, Library and Information Service, Reckitt and Colman Pharmaceutical Division, Hull, North Humberside HU8 7DS	A circular walk starting from near Fridaythorpe through a variety of contrasting scenery with impressive views.
Oxfordshire		
Oxfordshire Circular Walks (13 max.) **151, 164, 174, 175**	Oxfordshire County Council, Planning Dept, Macclesfield House, New Road, Oxford	Eight circular walks, 2 linking with the Ridgeway Path.
Oxfordshire Way (60) **163, 164, 175**	Council for the Protection of Rural England, Sandford Mount, Charlbury, Oxford OX7 3TL	From Henley-on-Thames to Bourton-on-the-Water linking the Chilterns and Cotswolds.
Staffordshire		
Staffordshire and Worcester Canal Footpath – see Hereford and Worcester		
Staffordshire Moorland (7 max.) **118, 119**	Chief Planning Officer, Staffordshire Moorlands District Council, New Stockwell House, Stockwell Street, Leek, Staffordshire	12 circular walks in the Staffordshire Moorlands, most linking with the Staffordshire Way.
Staffordshire Way (59) **118, 128**	Staffordshire County Council, County Planning Officer, County Buildings, Martin Street, Stafford ST16 2LE	Starts at Mow Cop on the rugged Congleton Edge, where it links with the Gritstone Trail, continues past Rudyard Lake, through the Churnet valley and across hilltop paths to Rocester. The second section runs from Rocester to Cannock Chase.
Somerset		
West Mendip Way (30) **182**	Tourist Information Centre, Beach Lawns, Weston-super-Mare	From the Bristol Channel coast at Uphill (south of Weston-super-Mare) along the Mendip Hills to Wells, passing Cheddar Gorge and Wookey Hole.
South Yorkshire		
Cal-der-Went Walk – see Derbyshire		
Surrey		
Greensand Way (12) **187**	Surrey Amenity Council, Jenner House, 2 Jenner Road, Guildford, Surrey GU1 3PN	Winterfield Heath to the Nower, Dorking; this is the middle section of a path which will follow the Greensand hills from Haslemere to the Kent border near Limpsfield, which is expected to be opened during 1981.

PATH NAME	ADDRESS FOR INFORMATION	DESCRIPTION
Tyne and Wear		
Derwent Walk – see Durham		
West Sussex		
Sussex Border Path – see East Sussex		
West Yorkshire		
Calderdale Way (50) **103, 104, 110**	West Yorkshire County Council, South Pennine Information Centre, Hebden Bridge, West Yorkshire	The path makes a circuit of Calderdale by way of Ripponden, Todmorden, Heptonstall, Brighouse and Greetland. There are many link paths, and the Pennine Way long-distance path is crossed twice.
Colne Valley Circular Walk (15) **110**	Colne Valley Society, 21 Station Lane, Golcar, Huddersfield HD7 4EG	A circular path from Golcar, Huddersfield, south-westward via Linthwaite, Lingards Wood, Butterley reservoir to Marsden, returning north of Slaithwaite over the moors; many linked circular paths.
Dales Way – see Cumbria		
Ebor Way – see North Yorkshire		
Leeds Country Way (65) **104**	Ian Kendall, Recreation and Arts Dept, West Yorkshire County Council, County Hall, Wakefield WF1 2QN	A circular path around Leeds, roughly 5 miles from the city centre, starting at Apperley Bridge and passing through delightful countryside, including the Harewood estate. It is intended to open several links with the city centre.
WALES		
Gwent		
Lower Wye Valley Walk (34) **162**	Gwent County Council, County Hall, Cwmbran, Gwent NP4 2XF	Follows the Wye valley from Chepstow to Ross. Provides a variety of views and interest in the Wye valley Area of Outstanding Natural Beauty.
Usk Valley Walk (22) **161, 171**	Gwent County Council, County Hall, Cwmbran, Gwent NP4 2XF	Follows Usk valley from Caerleon to Llanellen; several riverside stretches and superb views from high above the valley floor in the Wentwood section (between Usk and Caerlton).
Powys		
Glyndwr's Way (121) **125, 126, 135, 136, 148**	Powys County Council, Planning Dept, County Hall, Llandrindod Wells, Powys	A scenic path from Knighton to Welshpool, via Machynlleth; divided into 16 sections which vary from an easy walk to a strenuous climb.
Kerry Ridgeway (16) **136, 137**	Powys County Council, Planning Dept, County Hall, Llandrindod Wells, Powys	From Dollor, near Newton, along the west of the Kerry Hills to Bishops Castle.
Wye Valley Walk (36) **147, 148, 161**	Powys County Council, Planning Dept, County Hall, Llandrindod Wells, Powys	A scenic path from Hay-on-Wye to Rhayader, following or close to the River Wye; divided into 4 sections, all fairly easy going.
West Glamorgan		
Coed Morgannwg Way (26) **170**	Forestry Commission, District Office, London Road, Neath, West Glamorgan	From the scarp of Craig y Llyn (highest point in Glamorgan) to Margam Country Park via Afan Argoed Country Park, a forest path with spectacular views.
Fford y Brynian (21) (Ridgeway Walk) **170, 171**	Mr R. Clarke, Taff Ely Borough Council, 11–11A Mill Street, Pontypridd, Mid-Glamorgan	An upland path from Ogwr across Taff Ely to Caerphilly Common in Rhymney valley; magnificent views.

* Path open to horseriders and cyclists as well as walkers.

Country Parks

'Real country virtually on your doorstep' is the slogan the Countryside Commission uses to describe the numerous Country Parks scattered throughout Great Britain. The phrase is apt: country parks are secluded enclaves of woods or open parkland where you can walk, study the local natural history, or simply relax by absorbing the peace and beauty of the countryside. Some are quite small; others are spacious enough to contain facilities for fishing, sailing, riding and other outdoor pursuits.

For enthusiastic walkers the Country Parks have another, most valuable use – as pleasant areas in which to prepare for a long-distance walk and to keep reasonably fit between major expeditions. Those listed here all have a bridleway, footpath or nature trail where you can stretch your legs sufficiently to get the blood flowing again.

The acreage of each park is shown in brackets after each park name.

Area of Outstanding Natural Beauty has been abbreviated to AONB.

NAME Area (acres)	LOCATION	TERRAIN	FEATURES
ENGLAND			
Buckinghamshire			
Black Park (546)	4 miles north-east of Slough off north side of A412	woodland	lake, fishing, bridleways, canoeing, swimming, nature trail, model power boats
Cambridgeshire			
Ferry Meadows (494)	3 miles west of Peterborough city centre on A605 and A47	grassland	river Nene, nature trail, bridleways, sailing, rowing and fishing
Cheshire			
Lyme Park (1,323)	Disley, south-east of Stockport	wood and parkland	hall, orangery, deer, bridleways, putting, winter sports, nature trail, playground, gardens
Tatton Park (988)	1 mile north of Knutsford, 12 miles south-west of Manchester	park, wood and arable land	lake, sailing, fishing, swimming, picnic site, bridleways, medieval farm trail, Old Hall complex of house and gardens
Cornwall			
Mount Edgcumbe (759)	west of Plymouth	parkland on coast in AONB	views, gardens
Derbyshire			
Elvaston Castle (200)	6 miles south-east of Derby off B5010	wood and parkland	castle, lake, bridleways, nature trail, gardens, caravan/camping, playground
Hardwick Hall (250)	4 miles north-west of Mansfield adjoining M1	parkland	hall, lakes, fishing, canoeing, nature trail, gardens
Longshaw (1,381)	9 miles south-west of Sheffield off A625	meadow and woodland within Peak District National Park	rock climbing, nature trail, wildlife reserve, bridleways
Shipley (815)	access off A608 in Heanor and A6007 in Heanor-Ilkeston	meadow and woodland	bridleways, angling, nature trail, sailing
Dorset			
Durlston (262)	on coast south of Swanage	down and woodland, Heritage Coast in AONB	stone globe of the world, cliffs
Durham			
Derwent Walk (287)	between Swalwell and Consett	disused railway line undulating wooded valley	views, nature trails, bridleways
Waldridge Fell (284)	1 mile south-west of Chester-le-Street	heather moorland and bog	site of Special Scientific Interest
East Sussex			
Hastings (502)	east of Hastings on coast	wood, heath and meadow-land, foreshore, cliffs	fishing, boating, swimming, nature trails
Seven Sisters (445)	on coast between Seaford and Beachy Head off A259	down and marchland, saltings, Heritage Coast in AONB	visitor centre, bridleways, nature trail, fishing, canoeing
Essex			
Hatfield Forest (1,000)	4 miles east of Bishop's Stortford off A120	woodland	lake, boating, fishing
Marsh Farm (237)	1¼ miles south of South Woodham Ferrers	farm and marshland	river, farm, sailing, bird-watching, bridleways
Thorndon Park (353)	1½ miles south of Brentwood off A128	wood and meadowland	lake, fishing, bridleways
Weald Park (429)	1¾ miles north-west of Brentwood off A128	wood, meadow and parkland	lake, fishing, bridleways
Gloucestershire			
Robinswood Hill (240)	southern edge of Gloucester	wooded hill	views, bridleways, nature trails
Greater London			
Hainault Forest (1,095)	east of Chigwell off B174	wood and grassland	lake, pony and foal enclosures, bridleways, fishing, golf
Havering (166)	west of Havering-atte-Bower on B175	wood and parkland	bridleways
Trent Park (680)	1½ miles west of Enfield off A111	wood and parkland	lake, fishing, golf, bridleways

COUNTRY PARKS

NAME Area (acres)	LOCATION	TERRAIN	FEATURES
Greater Manchester			
Etherow (162)	3 miles east of Stockport	wood and marshland, river valley	reed beds and fish ponds, views, nature reserve, rowing, canoeing, nature trail
Haigh Hall (371)	1¾ miles north-east of Wigan	wood and heathland	lake, fishing, nature trail, arboreta, miniature golf, miniature zoo, children's playground, road train
Hampshire			
Farley Mount (263)	5 miles west of Winchester	wood and downland	views, Roman road, earthworks, bridleways
Queen Elizabeth (1,145)	1¾ miles south of Petersfield on A3	wooded hillside	views, bridleways, forest walks, grass ski-ing, Iron Age Farm
Wellington (598)	6¾ miles south of Reading near junction of A33 and A32	wood, heath and meadowland	lake, water sports, fishing, nature trail, playground, bridleways
Yateley Common (493)	1¾ miles west of Camberley off A30	heathland	ponds, fishing, bridleways, picnic sites
Hereford and Worcester			
Clent Hills (371)	8 miles west of Birmingham	hilly grassland	views, bridleways
Kingsford (215)	Kinver Edge 3 miles north of Kidderminster	wood and heathland	views, nature trail, waymarked walks with rail for disabled, waymarked bridleways
Lickey Hills (526)	8 miles south of Birmingham	wood, heath and meadowland	views, bird sanctuary, bridleways, boating, golf, ski-ing and tobogganing when conditions are suitable
Hertfordshire			
Great Wood (247)	5 miles south-east of Hatfield on B157	woodland	bridleways, route-marked walks
Knebworth (190)	1½ miles south-west of Stevenage	wooded parkland	house and gardens, playground, bridleways
Humberside			
Burton Constable (200)	8 miles north-east of Hull	hall with parkland	museum, lake, animals, fishing, swimming, bridleways, sailing/canoeing, rowing, bird-watching, nature trail, camping
Normanby Hall (168)	east of Normanby	house in wooded parkland	lake, museum, zoo, nature trail, squash, shooting, fishing, putting, archery, deer park, caravan/camping, bridleways, playground, gardens
Kent			
Eastcourt Meadows (907)	Lower Rainham Road, Gillingham	grassland and scrub on estuary of river Medway	
Lancashire			
Witton Park (250)	west of Blackburn	heath and woodland	views, nature trails, bridleways
Wycoller (363)	south-east of Colne	heath, moor and grassland	ancient monument, nature trail, bridleways
Leicestershire			
Bradgate Park and Swithland Woods (741)	6¾ miles north-west of Leicester off B5327 at Newtown Linford, or off B5330	open wood and parkland in Charnwood Forest	house ruins, views, deer, nature trail, geological interest, bridleways
Merseyside			
Croxteth Park (514)	5 miles north-east of Liverpool	park and woodland	walks and walled garden
Norfolk			
Fritton lake (232)	3 miles south-west of Great Yarmouth	wood and grassland	lake, rowing, fishing
Sandringham (519)	8 miles north-east of Kings Lynn off B1440	wood and heathland	nature trail
North Yorkshire			
Brimhan Rocks (363)	2¼ miles east of Pateley Bridge off B6265	heath, moor and crags	rock climbing
Northamptonshire			
Daventry (209)	1 mile north of Daventry on B4036	grassland around reservoir	reservoir, nature trail, bird-watching, fishing
Irchester (200)	1¾ miles south-east of Wellingborough	re-afforested land	nature trail
Northumberland			
Cragside (900)	east of Rothbury	steep, rocky, wooded hillside	lakes, rhododendrons, woodland drives, historic house
Nottinghamshire			
Clumber Park (3,147)	2½ miles south-east of Worksop off A60	wood, grass and farmland	lake, fishing, cycle hire
Colwick (260)	1½ miles east of Nottingham	woodland and water	fishing, nature trail, water sports (work still in progress on part of park)
Holme Pierrepont (300)	1 mile east of Nottingham	restored gravel pits	river, international rowing course, water sports, fishing, riverside walk
Sherwood Forest (500)	access off B6034 north of Edwinstowe	oak forest, heath and grassland	Major Oak, visitor centre, cricket ground
Staffordshire			
Cannock Chase (2,690)	3 miles south-east of Stafford on A34	heath and woodland in AONB	views, bridleways, vehicular tracks
Highgate Common (283)	1¾ miles west of Kingswinford	heath and woodland	views, bridleways
Parkhall (368)	Weston Coyney, east of Stoke-on-Trent	originally derelict (sandstone) heathland and coniferous woodland	nature trail, information centre, fishing, model aircraft flying, golf course, views, bridleways

NAME Area (acres)	LOCATION	TERRAIN	FEATURES
Surrey			
Box Hill (581)	1½ miles north-east of Dorking off A24	wood and downland	views, bridleways
Frensham (969)	3 miles south of Farnham on A287	sandy heath and common land	ponds, boating, sailing, fishing, bridleways
Horton (245)	1 mile from Ewell West station	wood and grassland	
Warwickshire			
Coombe Abbey (289)	4 miles east of Coventry on A4114	woodland	abbey, lake, boating, fishing, nature trail, gardens, playground, bridleways
West Yorkshire			
Newmillerdam (240)	3 miles south of Wakefield on A61	woodland around reservoir	reservoir, rhododendrons, extensive network of footpaths, boating, wildlife
Penistone Hill (175)	west of Haworth, near Keighley	heath and moorland, historic stone quarries	Brontë country
SCOTLAND			
Fife			
Lochore Meadows (919)	Lochore, east of M90	parkland and loch	information centre, fishing, sailing, walks, picnic areas, nature reserve
Grampian			
Aden (214)	adjacent to Old Deer, 6 miles west of Peterhead	woodland estate	caravan/camp site, car parks, picnic areas, footpaths, bridleways
Haddo (180)	Methlick, 7 miles north-west of Ellon	woodland and parkland	lake, footpaths, picnic areas, information centre
Lothian			
Almondell and Calderwood (222)	East Calder, 10 miles west of Edinburgh	woodland and river valley	information centre, picnic areas, woodlands, nature trail, riverside walks, group camping area, barbecue site
Beecraigs (793)	2 miles south of Linlithgow	woodland and reservoir	information centre, trails, fishing, deer park, camping area, barbecue site, archery
John Muir (1,168)	immediately north-west of Dunbar	coast and estuary	beach, cliff top walk, walks, caravan/camp site, golf course
Vogrie (257)	10 miles south of Edinburgh on A68, 1 mile west of Pathhead on B6372	parkland and mixed woodland	facilities for walking and picnicking
Strathclyde			
Balloch Castle (200)	Loch Lomond, ½ mile north of Balloch, adjacent to B854	parkland and loch-shore	visitor centre, nature trail, car parking, footpaths, slipway
Calderglen (373)	A726, south-east of East Kilbride	linear park following Calder river	waterfalls, nature trail, footpaths, picnic sites, play areas, golf course
Castle Semple (341)	Lochwinnoch, Renfrewshire	water park	sailing, rowing, boat hire and launching ramp, picnic areas, walks, nature reserve
Culzean (576)	11 miles south-west of Ayr off A719	estate grounds and woodland	information centre, display, picnic areas, trails, Culzean Castle
Dean Castle (200)	north-east Kilmarnock, off B7038 Glasgow Road	park, farmland and mixed woodland	visitor centre, nature trail, picnic areas, riverside walks, castle and museum
Gleniffer Braes (1,186)	Paisley, off Gleniffer Road	hill land	nature trail, viewpoints, visitor centre, pony trekking, fishing, picnic areas
Palacerigg (633)	2 miles south-east of Cumbernauld	woodland and parkland	information centre, footpaths, bridleways, wildlife centre, picnic areas
Pollock (361)	south-west Glasgow, Pollockshaws Road	mature woodland and parkland	walks, terraced garden, restored mill, Pollock House (Burrell art collection)
Strathclyde (1,601)	adjacent to M74 between Motherwell and Hamilton	parkland and large loch	international rowing course, sailing, park centre, picnic areas, caravan/camp site, nature trails/nature reserve
WALES			
Clwyd			
Erddig Park (206)	1 mile south-west of Wrexham	parkland and woodland	house and parkland, picnic sites, river, industrial trail, agricultural museum
Moel Famau (2,375)	6 miles west of Mold	moorland in Clwydian Hills	views, reservoir, Jubilee Tower, hill fort, Offa's Dyke
Dyfed			
Llys-y-frân Reservoir (308)	7½ miles north-west of Haverfordwest	wooded valley in foothills of Prescelly mountains	reservoir and dam, fishing, boating, nature trail, picnic sites
Gwynedd			
Padarn (320)	east of Llanberis	wood and heathland, disused quarry	lake, museum, railway, views, nature trail, picnic sites, boating, fishing
Mid Glamorgan			
Dare Valley (477)	west of Aberdare	open moorland, wooded valley	pools and waterfalls, industrial archaeology, playground, picnic sites
South Glamorgan			
Porthkerry Park (225)	1 mile west of Barry	wooded valley ending at sea shore	beach, water sports, pitch and putt, woodland trail, picnic sites
West Glamorgan			
Margam Park (795)	east of Port Talbot	park and woodland	orangery, castle, abbey, lakes, picnic areas, interpretation, park and ride service

Useful Addresses

The Backpackers Club, 20 St Michael's Road, Tilehurst, Reading, Berkshire RG3 4RP (National Organizer, Eric Gurney)

The Camping Club of Great Britain & Ireland Ltd, 11 Grosvenor Place, London SW1W 0EY; Northern England office (Association of Cycle and Lightweight Campers) 22 Holmsley Field Lane, Oulton, Leeds

The Caravan Club, East Grinstead House, East Grinstead, West Sussex RH19 1UA

The Council for the Protection of Rural England, 4 Hobart Place, London SW1W 0HY

The Council for the Protection of Rural Wales, 14 Broad Street, Welshpool, Powys SY21 7SD

The Countryside Commission, John Dower House, Crescent Place, Cheltenham, Gloucestershire GL50 3RA

The Countryside Commission for Scotland, Battleby, Redgorton, Perth, Tayside PH1 3EW

The English Tourist Board, 4 Grosvenor Gardens, London SW1W 0DU

The Forestry Commission, 231 Corstophine Road, Edinburgh EH12 7AT

Her Majesty's Stationery Office, 49 High Holborn, London WC1V 6HB (postal address PO Box 569, London SE1 9NH)

Her Majesty's Stationery Office (Scotland), 13A Castle Street, Edinburgh 2

Her Majesty's Stationery Office (Wales), 41 The Hayes, Cardiff

The National Trust, 42 Queen Anne's Gate, London SW1H 9AS

The National Trust for Scotland, 5 Charlotte Square, Edinburgh EH2 4DU

The Ordnance Survey Department, Romsey Road, Maybush, Southampton SO9 4DH

The Ramblers' Association, 1–5 Wandsworth Road, London SW8 2LJ

The Scottish Tourist Board, 23 Ravelston Terrace, Edinburgh EH4 3EU

The Wales Tourist Board, Brunel House, 2 Fitzalan Road, Cardiff CF2 1UY

The Youth Hostels Association, Trevelyan House, 8 St Stephen's Hill, St Albans, Hertfordshire AL1 2DY

Bibliography

The long-distance paths

B. Cowley, *The Cleveland Way*, Dalesman Publishing Company

A. Falconer, *The Cleveland Way*, Her Majesty's Stationery Office

C.J. Wright, *The Pilgrims Way and North Downs Way*, Constable

J.B. Jones, *Offa's Dyke Path*, Her Majesty's Stationery Office

A. Roberts, *Offa's Dyke Path*, Ramblers' Association

F. Noble, *The Shell Book of Offa's Dyke Path*, Queen Anne Press

T. Roberts, *A Guide to Walking the Pembrokeshire Coast Path*, Pembrokeshire Handbooks

J.H. Barrett, *The Pembrokeshire Coast Path*, Her Majesty's Stationery Office

T. Stephenson, *The Pennine Way*, Her Majesty's Stationery Office

A. Wainwright, *The Pennine Way Companion*, Westmorland Gazette, Kendal

M. Marriott, *The Shell Book of the Pennine Way*, Queen Anne Press

S. Jennett, *The Ridgeway Path*, Her Majesty's Stationery Office

H.D. Westacott, *The Ridgeway Path*, Footpath Publications

S. Jennett, *The South Downs Way*, Her Majesty's Stationery Office

Eastbourne Rambling Club, *Along the South Downs Way*

E.C. Pyatt, *The Cornwall Coast Path*, Her Majesty's Stationery Office

B. Jackman, *The Dorset Coast Path*, Her Majesty's Stationery Office

M. Marriott, *The Shell Book of the South-West Peninsula Path*, Queen Anne Press

B.Le Messurier, *The South Devon Coast Path*, Her Majesty's Stationery Office

K. Ward and J. Mason, *The South-West Peninsula Coast Path* (three volumes), Letts

R. Aitken, *The West Highland Way*, Her Majesty's Stationery Office.

Further Recommended Reading

R. Adshead and D. Booth, *Backpacking in Britain*, Oxford Press

S. Styles, *Backpacking in Wales*, Robert Hale

A. Wainwright, *A Coast to Coast Walk (Whitehaven to Whitby)*, Westmorland Gazette, Kendal

Dartmoor National Park, Her Majesty's Stationery Office

Explore the New Forest, Forestry Commission

A. Rowland, *Hillwalking in Snowdonia*, Cicerone Press

J. Hillaby, *Journey through Britain*, Granada

The Lake District National Park, Her Majesty's Stationery Office

B. Cowley, *The Lyke Wake Walk*, Dalesman Publishing Company

North York Moors National Park, Her Majesty's Stationery Office

Peak District National Park, Her Majesty's Stationery Office

J. Merrill, *The Peakland Way*, Dalesman Publishing Company

R.A. Redfern, *Rambles in Peakland*, Robert Hale

D.G. Moir, *Scottish Hill Tracks*, John Bartholomew

Snowdonia National Park, Her Majesty's Stationery Office

P. Lumley, *Spur Book of Hilltrekking*, Spurbooks

T. Brown and R. Hunter, *Spur Book of Map & Compass*, Spurbooks

M. Marriott, *Start Backpacking*, Stanley Paul

A. Greenbank, *Walking, Hiking & Backpacking*, Constable

Index

Acknowledgements

Aerofilms: 20 (above)
Barnaby's Picture Library: 18–9, 19, 42 (left), 48–9, 56–7, (above), 60, 65, 66 (above), 67 (above), 108, 117 (below), 119 (above), 149, 150
Janet & Colin Bord: 18, 30, 36 (above), 38, 47, 62 (both), 82–3, 84 (below), 103 (both), 110 (above), 110–1, 112, 139, 145
British Tourist Authority: 70, 71 (above), 82 (above), 86 (above), 91 (below), 94 (below), 94–5, 123 (above), 127 (below), 131 (bottom), 135 (above), 158
J. Allan Cash: 6, 7, 8, 11 (centre), 24–5, 25, 26 (above), 27, 29, 31 (both), 32–3, 33, 34–5, 35 (below), 37, 38–9, 42 (right), 43, 44, 45 (below), 46, 50 (below), 56–7 (below), 58, 58–9, 64–5, 66 (below), 72 (below), 74, 76–7, 79, 80, 80–1, 84 (above), 88, 90–1 (above), 91 (above), 92, 93, 96–7, 100–1, 104–5 (above), 107, 110 (below), 111, 113, 114–5, 115 (both), 117 (above), 119 (below), 121, 133 (centre & bottom), 137, 138, 140, 141, 142, 143, 148, 152, 153, 154–5, 155 (both), 160, 162
Cheze-Brown: 163
England Scene: 50–1, 78, 86 (below), 134–5, 146, 159
English Tourist Board: 74–5, 83 (below), 90–1 (below), 94 (above), 127 (above), 157
Fay Goodwin: 1, 3 (right), 4–5, 10, 17, 22–3, 23 (above), 123 (below), 124–5
International Scene Library: 54–5
Michael Marriott: 11 (top & bottom), 12, 13 (both), 14 (both), 15 (both), 20 (below), 21, 22, 23 (below), 35 (above), 36 (below), 39, 40–1, 45 (above), 49 (both), 50 (above), 53, 54 (both), 61, 67 (below), 71 (below), 72 (above), 73, 76 (both), 82 (below), 83 (above), 87, 96, 98–9, 99 (all), 106–7, 126 (above), 129 (above), 131 (top & centre), 133 (top), 135 (below), 151, 161, 164, 165 (both)
Picturepoint: 26 (below), 130–1
Department of Tourism and Amenities, Scarborough: 104–5 (below)
Spectrum Colour Library: 129 (below) (Robert Rixon)
Patrick Thurston: 102–3, 122, 147
Susan Vaillant: 2–3
Wales Tourist Board: 63, 118
Yorkshire and Humberside Tourist Board: 126 (below)

The maps were specially commissioned for this book. They were based upon Ordnance Survey maps with the permission of the Controller of Her Majesty's Stationery Office, Crown copyright reserved.
   The author and publishers gratefully acknowledge the co-operation and assistance of the Countryside Commission in many aspects of the production of this book. Also, Dr Robert Aitken who contributed the section on The West Highland Way.